WI Calendar of Feasts

Maggie Black

WI Books London

WI Calendar of Feasts
was edited and directed by
Imogen Bright, 21 Weeden Lane,
Amersham, Bucks.

Designers Anthony Lawrence & Hilly Beavan
Cover drawing Rodney Shackell

First published in Great Britain by WI Books Ltd.,
39 Eccleston Street, London SW1W 9NT, 1985

British Library Cataloguing in Publication Data
Black, Maggie
   W I calendar of feasts.
   1. Festivals—Great Britain
   I. Title
   394.2′0941   GT4843

ISBN 0 900556 93 5

Typeset by Burgess & Son (Abingdon) Ltd.
Printed and Bound in Hong Kong by Mandarin Offset Ltd.

AUTHOR'S NOTE

A good many people, myself included, believe that the old lore of farmland and homestead still has much to teach us about how to make the most of our natural world and to use its products well.

Most of us, however, have forgotten the old myths which used to account for the changing cycle of birth, growth, ripening and death, in nature as in human lives. We have forgotten, too, how the customs which embodied them used to vary from county to county as much as the climate and the foods which the local soil sustained.

Many of those customs have died out. Most which have survived have changed in form, and many of their old meanings have been lost. Others are being revived in modern forms, which have a new real meaning for us today.

More could be. I have suggested one or two in this book, and I hope that readers will find other customs which they can adapt to their local needs.

I have found it fascinating to trace these varying stories and customs, and I wish that I had been able to use all the material which members of the Women's Institute so kindly sent me. I hope I shall be forgiven for any special local features I have omitted, and any errors of fact I have made. I hope too that members may be stimulated to record and send in more local material so that one day we can make a more comprehensive book.

I should like to thank the WI immensely for this chance to explore and write about some aspects of Britain's food folklore, because I am sure that this heritage is worth preserving as a whole.

M.K.B. London. 1984.

3

THE NEW YEAR

Bringers of Good Luck

To many people, especially in the North and West, Christmas is still primarily a religious festival, and the real secular holiday with its remnants and reminders of more ancient pagan rites is New Year's Day.

A good example of this is the widespread custom of First-Footing. Southerners tend to think of it as a Scottish rite, but it is by no means exclusively so, and even in Scotland it takes different forms in different places. In essence the practice means that the first living soul (The First Foot) to enter a dwelling on New Year's morning 'lets the New Year in', and so determines the fortunes of everyone and everything within those four walls for the coming year.

The personal attributes of the First Foot, or Lucky Bird as some Northerners call him, largely determine the quality of the luck. Ideally he should be male, young, strong, good-looking, dark-haired with well-spaced brows, clear speech and a well-arched foot. The worst possible luck would be brought if the First Foot were an elderly, red-haired female with a squint, a hare lip and flat feet. In fact the First Foot is usually a male relative or known visitor of average looks.

The First Foot never comes empty-handed, because that would presage poverty or worse for his host. He comes bearing traditional symbolic gifts. The most usual are a piece of bread, a piece of coal or peat and a little salt, representing man's basic needs for food, warmth and wealth. In some parts of Scotland a bowl of ale caudle or a bottle of whisky is thought a necessity of life, and in some fishing areas a red herring as the longest-lasting preserved fish is offered. Often the First Foot brings evergreens such as mistletoe too, as a symbol of life's continuance.

As bearer of the coming year's fortune, the First Foot must be well entertained with food and drink. In Scotland whisky is the tipple, with the first slice of the traditional Black Bun. This very rich fruit cake is older in style than the Southerner's Christmas Cake. It is in fact more like the dough-crusted raised pies from which both cakes derive.

In Yorkshire until recently, as soon as the Lucky Bird had made his offerings, the householder would cut a cake and offer him the first slice together with a glass of wine. Toasts would then be drunk and the luck-bringer would be given symbolic gifts of cheese (as a milk preserve), a slice of ginger or rice cake (as grain and sweetness) and a coin or two.

In North Northumberland children used to go begging for a gift of small cakes called a Hogmanay. In parts of Wales these New Year Cakes and pennies are still called a Calennig. In Conventry people eat triangular Godcakes on New Year's Day, and in St. Albans small yeast buns called Pope Ladies, shaped like gingerbread men without legs, are still sold.

Dydd Calan

In Wales Dydd Calan or New Year's Day has always been a great day for secular festivity. Well into the last century, Dydd Calan was the traditional day for the main midwinter feast of goose boiled with parsley and onions, potato pudding baked a rich brown, and a generous skimmed milk rice pudding. Cinio Calan, or New Year Dinner, was a feast for stalwarts.

However, the chief feature of the Welsh New Year was a visit from the Mari Lwyd, a mock horse figure, which visited householders as a luck-bringer. Once a familiar feature of the midwinter festival in many widely-separated areas from Yorkshire to Kent, it now only

Guisers enjoying a dance.

bells were held by the Leader of five or six attendants in beribboned costume.

When the Leader knocked on anyone's door, he would call out for the chance to sing. Then followed a light-hearted exchange in verse. This continued until inspiration failed, and it was usually the householder who stopped first in order to allow the Mari Lwyd in. Once inside rhymes gave way to horse-play in every sense of the word, as the mock horse reared and stamped and pretended to bite everyone in sight. The hosts provided food and drink, and, this being Wales, probably everyone provided a fine song. Finally the horse and his attendants would depart singing a rhymed Welsh call for God's blessing on all within the house.

Here is Vernon Watkins' romantic modern version of the Mari Lwyd mummers' claim to entry and of the supper which might await them:

> *There were jumping sausages, roasting*
> *pies,*
> *And long loaves in the bin,*
> *And a stump of Caerphilly to rest our eyes,*
> *And a barrel rolling in.*
> *O a ham-bone high on a ceiling hook*
> *And a goose with a golden skin,*
> *And the roaring flames of the food you*
> *cook:*
> *For God's sake let us in.*

survives with its original comic mock savagery and rhyming repartee in a few places in Wales.

In the past, the Mari Lwyd in full trappings was a fine figure of a creature, and not a little scary to meet at one's front door at dusk. There before one was a horse's skull, real or wooden, with hinged jaws which snapped and bit, globes of glass as eyes and tall ears. Below the mask, a long sheet draped an unseen figure, in fact a strong local fellow. Reins jingling with

Highland hospitality.

January 1

January 8

January 2

January 9

January 3

January 10

January 4

January 11
Old New Year's Day

January 5

January 12

January 6
Twelfth Day

January 13
St. Agnes

January 7

January 14

OLD TWELFTH NIGHT & TWELFTH DAY

The mediaeval Christmas holiday ended with Twelfth Night ceremonies which dated back beyond Roman times and recalled the more ancient Winter Solstice rites. On West Midland farms the farmer and his men would light a large bonfire encircled by twelve smaller bonfires and on the highest point in a field sown with wheat. There they would drink toasts to make the harvest fruitful. In Herefordshire and Worcestershire they then went to the oxen and toasted them by name in strong ale, placing a plum cake in a ring shape on the horn of the finest ox. If he tossed it off forwards without being goaded, the farm would do well that year. The men would return to the farmhouse without any light to guide them, and had to sing for their supper before they were let inside.

In courtly circles Twelfth Day ceremonies were Roman in origin. The focus of the day was a feast at which the last of the Christmas boar or pig meat (the head) was garnished and served ceremoniously. A large rich plum cake was shared out, and whoever found a dried bean in his piece became King or Lord of Misrule for the all-night revels, and dictated what form the fun should take. This cake ceremony became more elaborate as time passed. Samuel Pepys records finding a clove —mark of the Knave— in his piece and hiding it in someone else's. By the late eighteenth century a Twelfth Cake had become a rich fruit mixture iced and decorated with vivid sugar flowers, gold stars and crowns, angels and figures of the Three Kings at Bethlehem. Well into this century the shops were full of special cakes, and a modern version containing the bean is still made in Cumberland. It would be good to revive the idea of a Twelfth Cake as an alternative to the Christmas Cake, and its design would offer a lot more scope to keen cooks.

PLOUGH SUNDAY & MONDAY

On the Sunday after Twelfth Day mediaeval farmers, free labourers and serfs cleaned and decorated their ploughs. Then they hauled them to church to be blessed, and to pray for a good harvest before the start of the new season's work. During the service the Plough Light, a candle kept lit in the church throughout the year, was paraded ceremonially.

The Sunday service was abandoned at the Reformation, but in recent years services of blessing for farm work and tools have been revived in some places, and it has been suggested that allotment holders and gardeners could hold their own similar services.

Top right: Procession of the Plough.

Spring ploughing started on Plough Monday.

On the following day spring ploughing would begin, provided that there was no frost. But work was not taken very seriously and finished early. There was a prize to be won. If the returning ploughman could call to his master 'cock in the pot' before the dairymaid could call 'cock on the dunghill', then the farmer would give the ploughman his traditional gift of a cockerel.

In the afternoon the young men of the village dressed up in white with horse brasses, bells and ribbons. Calling themselves Jacks or Stots—names for plough bullocks—they hauled a decorated plough all round the village, accompanied by mummers or Sword Dancers. A man dressed as a woman demanded money from every householder or passer-by as a contribution towards keeping the Plough Light alight in the church throughout the year. Anyone who refused to give had his doorstep ploughed up, or was roughly handled.

Some of these Plough Monday customs survived until recently. At Revesby in Lincolnshire there was a mummers' play, and at a village near Whitby the Plough Stots performed a dance thought to have been brought over by Norsemen over a thousand years ago. In other places a Straw Bear was taken around the village to sing. At Balsham in Cambridgeshire Plough Monday has been revived, and ploughboys, wearing assorted costumes offer a singing and dancing entertainment for charity, much in the old style.

In the past, the day ended with a village feast. Ale or beer flowed, and the traditional centrepiece was always a large Plough Pudding, preceded by a substantial root vegetable and meat stock pottage, and followed by Plum Pottage (a meaty muesli-type mixture which in later times became Plum Pudding). Several recipes for Plough Pudding survive, the best known being the one from Sussex. It would be pleasant to wish the year's work fruitful by organizing a 'Soup (or pottage) and Pudding' party where the centre-piece is a Plough Pudding. This would be, not only original, but also a simple and economical entertainment.

ST AGNES' FAST

St. Agnes, who was only thirteen years old when she was martyred, became immensely popular as the patron saint of all young girls who dreamed of a perfect marriage. In the North Country, especially throughout Durham, there was a special ritual on St. Agnes Eve. A pair of girls who wanted to dream of their future spouses had to abstain from food, drink and speech all that day. At night they made a Dumb Cake (doughy flatbread) with ingredients provided by their friends, who also had to take equal shares in baking and turning the cake and in removing it from the oven. The cooked cake was halved, and each girl had to carry her share to bed walking backwards, eat it and jump into bed. The solid dough supper after fasting and brooding on the ideal husband all day might well make any girl have dreams.

In nearby Northumberland they had other ways of stimulating the desired dreams. Here girls ate hard-boiled eggs, shell and all, filled with salt in place of the yolks. In fishing villages they might choose a salty raw red herring complete with its bones. Indigestion is a great aid to magic!

January 15

January 16

January 17
Old Twelfth Day

January 18

January 19

January 20

January 21

January 22

January 23

January 24

January 25
Conversion of St. Paul

January 26

January 27

January 28

CANDLEMAS

Candlemas was the most unshadowed, serenely hopeful feast of the pre-Reformation church. Like almost all such feasts, its meaning goes further back than Christianity. Candles have been symbolic of life and resurrection since ancient times, and therefore closely associated with returning spring and the growth of crops and creatures. In the days of the early church Candlemas, being the end of the Church's Christmastide and of winter, was the time when people's thoughts turned to spring.

From the eleventh century the Church's candles for the coming season were paraded and consecrated at Candlemas. These were always costly real beeswax candles, because tradition held that bees came from Heaven. The procession and blessing of candles at this time went back to the pagan torch processions which had wound about the fields bringing light to invigorate the soil before the spring sowing.

Being the only form of domestic lighting, cheaper tallow candles and rushlights had scores of superstitions attached to them. According to the flame's colour or how it flickered, they would foretell who would live, prosper, marry or die during the year. In some places the Yule Candle was relit for a family feast on Candlemas Night to mark the dedication of Spring. In Dorset, a large candle was often a gift, and the family would have cakes and ale or punch by its light until it went out. Children were allowed to stay up late on this night, if on no other.

But farming folk had to be practical too. February food was lean and February work hard. Thomas Tusser, the great verse recorder of the farming year, pointed out vigorously in

In spite of thoughts of spring, February work was hard.

12

his instructions for the months that if a man failed to till and to keep his working stock in good condition, *that* would impoverish both his land and himself, although marling and manuring were necessary as well. The farmer was to plough and to sow beans and peas to dry against the next winter. Mustard was to be sown in new-turned soil, and hemp seed sown to strangle nettles. Vines and osiers should be pruned and replaced if necessary, while land to be left for hay should now be manured. Barley for malt and seed corn should be threshed, except for a small quantity to give the labourers indoor work if the weather turned sour. Land should be fenced with hedges, and standing willows planted to shade the cattle.

Such end-of-winter tasks bring home vividly how closely every family in a society without shops depended on the new springing of seed and the rising of sap in the local fields. They also illustrate how deeply the folk rituals which accompanied them were embedded in the way of life of country people.

A FEBRUARY FEAST

On 7th February 1404 a royal feast was held at Winchester to celebrate the second marriage of King Henry IV to Joan of Navarre. As mediaeval feasts are almost legendary examples of extravagance, the menu for this one is worth glancing at. Although the three courses contained a total of thirty items (with a parallel fish menu for the clergy), we must remember that no one ever tried them all. At any feast five or six social groups were served, each having a different menu. The high table would have the grandest and the greatest number of dishes, while the lowliest groups had three or four dishes per course at most. In any case, a good many of the menu items were very small—woodcock, plover, quail, snipe, fieldfares and 'smale byrdes' would hardly make more than a mouthful each. Probably no one got more than two mouthfuls of such a dish, even at the top table.

However, the guests there had a wide choice of other delicacies such as baby swan, fat chickens and sucking-pig. Venison and game birds featured too, since it was still winter. As for sweet dishes, these were not served last in today's style, but were presented with the savoury dishes. At this marriage feast, the sweets included a stiff rice-flour cream, large stewed pears in wine, jelly, apple fritters, almond cream, cottage cheese tart or cheesecake and moulded marzipan sweets. All quite practical winter party fare for today!

ST VALENTINE

St. Valentine's Feast is not only notable for lovers. In Norfolk, especially around Norwich, St. Valentine's Eve was until recently a time of 'Knock and Run' secret gifts. These would be laid on the doorstep, the bell rung, and the donor would flee before the door opened. Gifts would vary from a single cake to costly jewellery, and the game was to guess who had sent them. Anyone might benefit, not just lovers.

Children also enjoyed St. Valentine's Day for another reason. A favourite East Anglian activity was to go round singing for alms before sunrise. The children would be given coins, fruit or special pastry cakes filled with chopped (presumable preserved) plums.

January 29

January 30
Charles I beheaded

January 31

February 1

February 2
Candlemas

February 3
St. Blaise

February 4

February 5

February 6

February 7

February 8

February 9

February 10

February 11

SHROVETIDE

Shrovetide has more surviving customs and local happenings, and more names for them than any other Church season except Christmas. This is probably because in mediaeval times Lent was a rigidly strict fast, and this was the last chance for a good 'blow-out' for several weeks to come.

The days just before Lent had different names depending on where you lived, and what (or how much) you ate. The names Bursting Saturday, Bacon and Egg Sunday, Guttit Day and Bannock Day speak for themselves. On the Saturday, Lincolnshire folk used to make special thick crumbly pancakes. On Peasan Monday in Cornwall, they drank pea soup, but elsewhere in England eggs and fried bacon or mutton collops were eaten, hence the alternative name Collop Monday. In parts of Hertfordshire, Shrove Tuesday was called Doughnut Day because doughnuts fried in lard were popular, while in Norwich bakers made and sold shell-shaped currant cakes rather like French madeleines.

Shrove Tuesday was also known as Lincrook Day and Lentshard Night. These names probably came from the West Country custom of backing up demands for pancakes by throwing stones or bits of crockery against the house doors, if not bribed to move on.

In many places, it was the custom for poor women, in particular, to go from door to door seeking alms, usually foodstuffs to make a pancake feast for their children. They were known as Shrovers. Children too might be Shrovers, but they begged for a less serious reason. They would sing a Shrovetide begging song, a typical version being:

> A-shroving, a-shroving,
> We've come a-shroving,
> A bit of bread, a truckle of cheese,
> A bit of your fat bacon, please,
> Or a little pancake,
> Of your own making.

Westminster School's Pancake Greaze in London still takes place. It's origins are lost, but Jeremy Bentham the philosopher described it taking place in the 1750's, and it has not changed much since then, except that only one boy from each form now takes part, instead of the whole school. The pancake is brought into school at 11.00 a.m. by a procession of the Abbey Beadle with his mace, the Dean's Verger, the Dean and the Headmaster. At a signal the chef tosses the pancake over a high bar to the waiting boys. In the ensuing scramble or Greaze the boy with the largest bit of pancake is declared the winner and gets a golden guinea from the Dean (later exchanged for cash). Until 1860 no one got the guinea unless the pancake was secured whole. A modern development which shows how living folk traditions change is that the boys now wear fancy dress.

Pancake throwing at Westminster School.

The Pancake Race at Olney in Buckinghamshire is another much copied survival, dating back to 1445. Housewives of Olney and neighbouring Warrington, with their heads covered and wearing aprons, are eligible. Each carries a frying pan, complete with pancake, and must toss it three times during the race from Olney village square to the parish church where the vicar awaits them. The winner gets a prayer book as a prize. The verger claims a kiss from her, and the pans are then taken into the church to be blessed. Another popular Pancake Race is held at Winster in Derbyshire.

In Scotland, instead of pancakes 'Beef, brose and bannocks', so Christina Hole tells us, used to be the order of the day on Shrove Tuesday. Beef was thought to be essential at the farmer's dinner, or his cattle would not thrive. A fat brose (cow heel or shin and oatmeal broth) was served as the first dish, with charms in it, like the charms in a modern Christmas pudding and with the same meanings. In the evening, oatmeal girdle bannocks were made, with all the unmarried people present sharing

Bellringing was a signal to start pancake making.

the bannock would be lost and someone else would have to take over the making. When the bannock was ready, the cook cut it into as many pieces as there were unmarried people present, and each person took a portion containing a hidden charm. This was saved until bedtime, and then wrapped in a stocking and put under the pillow so that the sleeper would dream of his or her future spouse.

In Wales, there are almost as many names for pancakes as there are parishes, and as many ways of making them. Welsh cooks are known as unrivalled pancake makers.

Bell-ringing used to be widespread at Shrovetide. Originally it was intended to call people to go to pre-Lent confession, which was the main object of this short church season. Later it came to be a signal for pancake-making to begin.

Shrovetide was marked by many other customs, symbolizing a last cheerful fling before the season of penance. Ball games were particularly popular. Two well-known football games survive, one at Ashbourne in Derbyshire after a traditional lunch at the Green Man Hotel, the other at Corfe Castle in Dorset. In Cornwall at St. Columb and St. Ives there is a local variation of football known as Silver Ball Hurling. Following the game at St. Columb, the Silver Ball is taken round the pubs and dipped in a jug of bear to provide Silver Beer for all. Other sports included egg-shackling competitions in Cornwall and Dorset, bull-baiting on the Isle of Wight, and throwing at cocks in Hampshire and Staffordshire.

in the work whether they belonged to the family or not. When everyone had eaten as many hot bannocks as they could, the last and most significant bannock was cooked. This foretold the future. Most people know it best as the Sautie Bannock, although it had various other names. It was large and thick, had charms in it like the brose, and it had to be made by one cook in total silence. If anyone could make her speak or laugh, the magical properties of

Football was played in many places at Shrovetide.

February 12

February 19

February 13

February 20

February 14
St. Valentine

February 21

February 15

February 22

February 16

February 23

February 17

February 24
St. Matthias

February 18

February 25

LENTEN FARE

Throughout the Middle Ages the Lent fast was extremely strict—at least in theory. Meat, milk, eggs, cream and cheese were forbidden to all healthy adults. They also had to give up Friday night supper, and ideally breakfast on two days a week as well.

In fact, for the rich, Lenten fare was not too depressing. There were plenty of cunning, often amusing, ways to get round the ban on meat for instance. Beaver's tail, barnacle goose or puffins and other water birds, such as gulls and heronshews (baby herons), could be counted as fish. A rich man also had his own stewponds stocked with pike, carp, tench and other river fish. Alternatively, he could send to London for luxuries such as imported smoked salmon, sturgeon (a royal fish), botargo (salted cod's roe) or porpoise (the luxury Lenten substitute for venison).

As for other foods, his custards could be thickened with 'almond milk, boyled' and his fritters could be fried in sweet almond oil. Almonds also provided mock foods. A favourite idea was to fill blown eggshells with fine almond paste, part of it coloured yellow to represent the egg yolk, the rest left white.

Poor people, by contrast, fared sadly. The peasant's staple proteins, hard cheese and a bit of salt bacon, were forbidden fare. For him, Lent meant salt fish and short commons for six weeks on end, and this salt fish was almost inevitably herring or ling, as they were cheapest.

Even the rich, however, had to eat a good deal of salt fish. Not surprisingly, dozens of spicy herb sauces, often thickened with breadcrumbs, were devised by their mediaeval cooks to mask its taste. Our modern bread sauce and mint sauce are relics of those days. Parsley too was used abundantly with fish even then.

The restrictions did not cease when Henry VIII broke with the Roman Church. The government found that it still had to impose a fish diet in the old style. Meat was scarce and expensive, and also if the fishing fleet were not kept busy, England would lose her skilled shipbuilders and seamen, who were vital to her security. The Puritans enforced abstention even more strictly, and allowed soldiers to enter private houses and seize meat on fast days. It was perhaps this feature which made Puritan rule most unpopular, and led to a diminishing

Woman's work: cleaning the pans.

respect for Lenten fasting in the following century.

ST DAVID'S DAY

A modernised convivial but dignified ceremony still takes place on St. David's Day, not in Wales but in Oxford. In 1732 Sir Watkin Williams-Wynne, who was virtual proprietor of Denbighshire, presented a fine silver-gilt wassail bowl and matching ladle to Jesus College. The bowl was used until the late nineteenth century, when being too large for ornamental use, it was put into the College's silver store. It languished there until a few years ago when Mr. Richard Sharp revived this kindly tradition, not in Hall but in the Graduates' Common Room. The Principal attends and invites research students and undergraduates. The room is decorated with daffodils, and the Dyfydd ap Gwylym Society (The University Welsh speakers' club) joins the company after its St. David's Day dinner. The original drink called Swig is then drunk. This is made by dissolving sugar in warm beer, topping up with more beer, and lacing the brew with sherry and nutmeg before cooling it.

MOTHERING SUNDAY

Mothering Sunday or Simnel Sunday, (not the same as Mother's Day) was once a pleasant mid-Lent break. It arose from a church ordinance requiring priest and people to visit the Mother Church halfway through Lent. In 1644 one Richard Symonds described it as a 'great day' when all the children and god-children feasted with the head of their household. Later, until servants got regular holidays, Mothering Sunday was a day when young girls out in service visited their mother with a gift of a trinket or a posy of spring flowers, and received her blessing. At first, they would bring a wafer cake too.

The mother, however, always prepared a festive dinner. In Worcestershire, Staffordshire and Shropshire families would eat veal, in Gloucestershire veal or lamb, and in Devonshire lamb, while in Warwickshire a chine of pork might be served. The meat was followed by a rice, suet or (in Norfolk) plum pudding. In parts of Lancashire, Yorkshire and Staffordshire they would eat Fig Pie (called Fag Pie) and Frumenty, together with the ancient sweetened herb ale called Braggot.

In later times there developed the idea of having a Mothering or Simnel Cake as well. Several different forms of this cake were still made in the 1950's, the best known being those of Bury in Lancashire, Devizes and Shrewsbury. A Bury Simnel was a fruit mixture which looks like a mediaeval page's cap, being a flattish, slightly domed bun turned up at the edges. The star-shaped Devizes Simnel was an enriched saffron bread. The Shrewsbury one

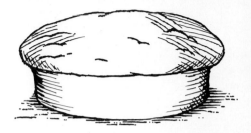

had a saffron bread crust enclosing a rich fruit mixture, and is reputed to have been boiled for some hours, and then baked until its crust was rock hard so that it would keep for a year like a Christmas Pudding. Its raised saffron bread rim surrounded decorative almond paste flowers, fruits and birds' eggs the size of sparrows' eggs.

Our modern Simnel cakes, usually eaten at Easter, owe more to the old aristocratic marchpanes and later plum cakes than to the wafer and bread-like Simnels described above. We have reduced the marchpane to a mere layer of marzipan in the centre of a fruit cake and another on top. The decorations too have now become just eleven small balls to represent all the apostles except Judas around the top and a larger ball in the centre to represent Christ.

Woman's work: cake-making.

February 26

March 4

February 27

March 5

February 28

March 6

February 29

March 7

March 1
St. David

March 8

March 2

March 9

March 3

March 10

DAYS OF DOLE

Doles or charitable distributions were vital in the days before the Welfare State. For the poorer members of the community these annual customs were a significant feature of the festival calendar. Several old bequests for instance lightened the sombre quality of Lent.

We know of two food charities that used to take place in Essex. At Saffron Walden, a certain William Leader left a sum to be spent on bread for the poor on the first Sunday in 'Cleane Lent', and at Clavering, one John Thame dictated in his will that a barrel of white herrings (pickled herrings) and a cade of red herrings (heavily salted herrings) should be given to the local poor each Lent. The Prior of Merton at Godmanchester in Huntingdonshire used to give 3 qrs of wheat, 3 qrs of rye and 1 qr of barley (1 quarter=8 bushels) to be distributed among the poorest parishioners.

The Tichborne Dole is one of Britain's most ancient folk benefits. The story goes that the twelfth century Lady Mabel de Tichborne tried to perpetuate her generous custom of alms-giving. On her deathbed she asked her ungenerous husband to set aside a piece of their Hampshire lands to grow corn for the poor. Taking a burning brand from the fire he told her that she might have as much land as she

Visiting the poor

could walk round before it died out. This was as good as a refusal to the dying woman, but Mabel was not deterred. Her gentlewomen carried her outdoors, and since she could no longer walk, she crawled around twenty-three acres before the brand flickered out. There is in fact a field at Tichborne still known as The Crawls. Triumphantly, the dying lady charged her husband to fulfil his side of the bargain and donate the produce of the land to the local poor 'for ever'. She warned that if ever the gift were withheld, the family would die out. It would be heralded by a generation of seven sons being

The Tichborne Dole, 1670.

followed by a generation of seven daughters, after which the line and the Tichborne name would fail. The manor house would also fall.

The dole was duly given annually until 1796, when Sir Henry Tichborne turned the income from The Crawls over to the church because wandering beggars abused the charity. Sir Henry did indeed beget seven sons. Four died without issue, and one had the threatened seven daughters. One of these had a son who died aged six, whereupon the bereaved father promptly changed his name and reinstated the dole. What power, if any, caused the prophecy to come true, and what would happen if it lapsed again, we do not know. But the dole has been given ever since, although it was threatened in the post-war days of bread rationing. Flour instead of loaves is now distributed on Lady Day after being blessed by the local priest.

By contrast, the Marvyn Charity is recent and meek, with no threat of doom from dying lips. In the church at Ufton Nervet in Berkshire there is a Table of Benefaction detailing the bequests of Dame Elizabeth Marvyn who was buried there in 1581, '10 bushels of wheat to be made into good household bread, 12½ ells of canvass at 1s per ell for shirts and smocks, and also 12½ yards of narrow blue cloth at 1s 8d per yard for coats and cassocks'. The gifts were to be charged against the profits from some of her lands, and were 'to be annually distributed about the middle of Lent'.

The distribution is still made from a downstairs window of Ufton Court, once Dame Elizabeth's home. About a hundred and fifty loaves are given to all parish residents, a loaf per head to the families of farm workers, a single loaf per household to others. The loaves are now white loaves. In Dame Elizabeth's day 'household bread' was second quality brownish bread given to the senior officials and servants of the house. The canvas and cloth dole has been transmuted into pairs of sheets given to nine old age parishioners of ten years' standing.

CARLIN SUNDAY

Passiontide starts on the fifth Sunday in Lent, a week after Mothering Sunday. It used to be called Care Sundy or Judica Sunday, and in the North of England and in Scotland the name Carling, Carlin or Carline is still used. Carlins are grey parched peas, and several tales are told

Giving to the poor.

of how they came to be Passion Sunday fare.

The most probable is that they are a hangover from an old pagan spring bean-feast held at this time. It is born out by the fact that in Northumberland a bean was hidden among the peas in the dish at dinner, and whoever got it would be the first to wed. Certainly it would be easy to hide, as the local way to serve Carlins is to boil the soaked peas, then fry them in butter and pour rum liberally over them.

Newcastle has its own story of the original link between carlins and Passion Sunday. During the Border Wars of the fourteenth century the Scots blockaded the city, and the people would have starved had not a French ship brought in a cargo of carlins under cover of darkness. Thereafter on this day pub-keepers gave away to each customers a quart of carlins. Newcastle's claims are somewhat disputable, as it was traditional to have free carlins on the house in many other North Country pubs.

One suspects that the real reason for eating Carlins late in Lent was sheer poverty. Spring came late, greenstuffs were few, and so dried foods were the rule at a time when dairy foods were forbidden. Also as Lent neared its end, the more flavoursome beans had probably been finished, and only the ashen peas were left.

March 11

March 18

March 12

March 19

March 13

March 20

March 14

March 21
St. Benedict

March 15

March 22

March16

March 23

March 17

March 24

HOLY WEEK

Palm Sunday

Magical beliefs about palms and Going Palming were held in England long after the Reformation, and have still not quite faded. Going Palming meant going to the woods to gather the boughs of the fine golden-catkined sallow willow. They were made into crosses, which were tacked to the house wall to protect it from demons, or which sometimes were thrown into wells to give the water curative powers and as a means of foretelling marriage or death.

In some parts of England, Palm Sunday was known Spanish Sunday. This was because children in the West Riding of Yorkshire filled bottles with water at a local well and then sweetened it with Spanish liquorice or peppermint candy. Children at Leafield in Oxfordshire also used to sweeten their well-water with Spanish liquorice.

Another name for Palm Sunday is Fig Sunday. This arose from the widespread custom of eating figs, especially Fig Pudding, to commemorate Christ having found no fare on the barren fig tree. Fig Pudding was the main dish at dinner in Hertfordshire around Watford, and has disappeared only as surburban conurbations and their shifting populations have swamped the patches of village green, and the leisurely village skills handed down from mother to daughter.

Elsewhere, one or two communal public festivities are recorded. At Kempton and on top of Silbury Hill in Wiltshire, villagers used to assemble to eat figs and to drink each other's health, usually in cider. On Dunstable Downs, crowds would gather to eat figs and fly kites.

Most crowd and parish events connected with Palm Sunday have lapsed. However, the distribution of Pax Cakes in Herefordshire is one pleasant survival. In the mid-seventeenth century, a certain Lady Scudamore decided to promote peace and friendship among the parishioners of Sellack, Kings Caple and Hentland, by instituting a communal meal in church. She and two others therefore gave to the Charity Commissioners 'a gift of 10s. per annum to be paid to the churchwardens to buy ale and cakes to be dealt in the church every Palm Sunday'.

At one time a single cake was made, but later small cakes were supplied instead, and handed round in baskets 'covered with a snowy white cloth'. In 1907, the Herefordshire Journal reported that these cakes had 'been the means of settling bitter feuds'—by no means the usual result of a pious legacy.

Maundy Thursday

Holy Week, the culmination of Lent, was a busy time of penitential and purifying washing in preparation for Easter. The house, cottage or croft had to be scrubbed inside and out, clothes washed as well as drapes, tablecloths and other linen. It is said to have been one of the origins of spring cleaning! People were also scrubbed, shaved—and deloused. As late as 1700, nits in one's hair were a matter of course. This explains why Maundy Thursday was also called Shere Thursday in some places.

The central English event of Maundy Thursday is the giving of the Royal Maundy, which has always been a great state occasion. *Maunds* was an old word for gifts, the sovereign exercising practical charity in the form of food and (at one time) clothing to the poor. Similar charities took place elsewhere. In the Cloisters at Durham the monks washed, dried and kissed the feet of poor children and then gave each one twenty silver pennies, seven dried herrings, three loaves of bread and a wafer cake.

The Maundy Thursday fair held at Tombland near Norwich shows how quick our forebears were to turn any group occasion into a shopping spree or treat, even on such a solemn day. The brown and white Buttons associated with the fair can still be purchased. The brown ones are gingerbread biscuits, flavoured with spice and chopped peel, and the white ones are flavoured with lemon.

Good Friday

Even today, devout Christians in the Eastern Church touch no food on Good Friday, while in Western Churches some families keep to the more relaxed, traditional 'reformed' diet of salt fish and vegetables, with figs or fig pudding afterwards. Fig Sue, an ale caudle boiled with breadcrumbs and sliced figs but no fat was once drunk too.

In some places, so far from fasting, special foods were eaten on Good Friday to commemorate the Last Supper, For example, scholars at Brasenose College, Oxford had almonds, raisins and figs, while in Devon and Cornwall, saffron buns and clotted cream were nineteenth century favourites. Easter Ledge or Passion Dock (bistort) Pudding still appears in North Country recipe books today. Easter Ledges, tansy and saffron were featured for their sharp flavour, in memory of the bitter herbs eaten by the Jews at Passover and given to Christ on the Cross.

For most of us Good Friday would lack something without Hot Cross Buns. Small wheaten buns and 'cakes' were eaten by several early peoples to celebrate the Spring Equinox. Like all treat foods and drinks, the buns were often spiced, and the tops were slashed with a cross to help them rise.

By Christian times it had become quite common to break off small parts of the bread dough before baking a batch of loaves for a feast day, to make small spiced buns as a modest treat. At the same time, superstitions developed about the cross-cuts on the top of the loaves. Although in fact the ale yeast used in the past was unreliable, if bread did not rise, it was believed that the devil lurked inside. It was also said that crosses prevented witches dancing on the dough and the Devil sitting on the bread or buns in the oven.

Bread for Easter Day was baked on Good Friday. This holy bread was baked with special care, and it was natural to superstitious minds that it should be protective, not only against devils, but also the ills of the flesh, from fevers to foot and mouth disease. Hence one Good Friday bun or loaf of the batch would be baked hard and dry, and then hung up. If grated into milk or a caudle, it was a foolproof cure for men and beasts alike. Nor would it ever lose its power!

After the Reformation, the new Protestant beliefs decreed that crosses, even on bread, were popish superstition. However, it was impossible to break the Good Friday link with the idea of magical holiness, and this seems to be the reason why Good Friday buns alone have kept their crosses, along with their curative reputation. The latter lingers still. At a Leicestershire radio phone-in programme in 1983, several listeners described their hundred-year-old Hot Cross Buns and the 'cures' for which their mothers had used them.

Holy Week was a time for washing clothes and household linens.

March 25
The Annunciation

March 26

March 27

March 28

March 29

March 30

March 31

April 1
All Fools' Day

April 2

April 3

April 5

April 4

April 6

April 7

EASTERTIDE

Easter Eggs

Eggs are one of man's oldest symbols of continuing life, and so they have always been revered as images. Sadly, in England we have almost lost the art of decorating hard-boiled eggs with multi-coloured patterns. In Cumberland they still wrap eggs in leaves, flowers, onion skins and brightly coloured materials.

Before the Reformation, eggs were brought to church at Easter to be blessed. Simple folk believed that the eggs thus became safeguarding charms or could be used in cures or for marriage divining. Even today, one occasionally finds Pace Eggs—the North Country name for paschal eggs—which have been kept as good luck charms for many years.

Playing games with dyed eggs used to be common all over England at Eastertide. One amusing tale describes how the Bishop and Dean of Chester took eggs to the cathedral and had an egg-throwing match with the choristers during the service, after which they all went off to dine together on gammon and tansy pudding. Possibly the oldest game was egg-rolling, which is still popular in the North Country. Indeed most towns and villages in the Lake District once had a special Pace Egg-Rolling site. In Carlisle in the 1850's crowds used to assemble to roll thousands of dyed hard-boiled eggs down a grassy slope until they cracked. They were then of course eaten.

Egg-rolling may have started, like Cheese-rolling, as a rite symbolizing worship of the returning sun and spring. Sometimes, especially in Scotland, the eggs were used for divination. If an egg reached the bottom of the slope unbroken, its owner would have good luck. Alternatively, boys and girls might roll their eggs separately. The two youngsters whose eggs rolled furthest would marry first.

At Preston in Lancashire, oranges are rolled with the eggs, which may be a revival of an ancient sun-image.

Egg-shackling is another game to survive.

An Easter family dinner was a time of rejoicing.

32

It is played like Conkers, except that the eggs are held in the hand, not swung on a string.

Easter Foods

Unfortunately we have forgotten many of the special Easter dishes which once celebrated the feast of the Resurrection. This is a pity, because a traditional Easter dinner is a reminder that the new seasonal foods were once a reason for real rejoicing after a sparse winter diet.

Fresh spring herbs featured largely in all dishes. Tansy juice, for instance, was used in an egg dish rather like scrambled eggs, which was called a herbolace or simply a tansy. As time went on, less and less of the herb was included, and eventually the name Tansy came to mean a sweet rich omelet, often including apples, but no tansy at all! Some other favourite Eastertime herbs were mint, parsley and sage. These were served with the new spring lamb, porkling and soft green (unmatured) cheeses.

Egg dishes and cream from the new rich spring milk were also festive fare. At Whitby in Yorkshire, baked custard was a traditional dish, and the prevailing spring wind was called 'the custard wind'. Custards were also popular in East Anglia. In Hertfordshire and Warwickshire cheesecakes were the thing. Barnet cheesecakes were praised in 1667 by Samuel Pepys. As for meats, people in Shropshire ate leg of pork stuffed with 'Robin-run-i'-the-hedge', and in Sussex everyone ate Southdown lamb, while bobby veal was popular in the North and the Midlands.

Other Easter dishes were pies of aloes, figs and radishes. Easter cakes and biscuits were eaten everywhere, but especially in the West Country. These curranty Easter biscuits still appear in most standard recipe books. In Kent pudding-pies are still made, which are flat tarts with a raised crust, containing custard sprinkled with currants.

Easter Games

Many Easter games were connected with the Easter Hare, once sacred to Eostre, the pagan goddess of Spring. Children are still told that Easter Eggs are laid by the Easter Bunny.

The Hallaton Bottle-Kicking and Hare Pie Scramble in Leicestershire is as popular now as it was when it began centuries ago. No-one knows how the custom started. However, land was bequeathed to the rector provided that he and his successors supplied every year two Hare Pies, a quantity of ale and twenty-four penny loaves to be scrambled for each Easter Monday at Hare Pie Bank. The Hare Pies may once have been made of hare meat. If so, it would point to a very ancient origin instead, but the Pies may only be so named because they were originally distributed at a spot called Hare Crop Leys.

Today, following a church service and refreshments at the Village Hall, a parade marches to the church gates where the pies (beefsteak) are cut up and half (1977) or all (1983) of the pieces are distributed. Then, at the Fox Inn, three 'bottles' are decorated with red, white and blue ribbons. Two of these are small wooden barrels, iron-hooped and filled with ale. The third is a dummy. When the parade reaches Hare Pie Bank, any remaining pie is scrambled for and the bottle-kicking contest—a kind of free-for-all football—takes place between the villagers of Hallaton and of neighbouring Medbourne.

Nowadays outsiders join in, and the whole occasion can get quite rough. But it is an excellent way to raise funds for charity.

April 8

April 15

April 9

April 16

April 10

April 17

April 11

April 18

April 12

April 19

April 13

April 20

April 14

April 21

ST GEORGE'S DAY

The history of St. George has no English roots at all. England's patron saint was a wealthy young Christian born in Palestine towards the end of the third century, who became a Roman military tribune and was martyred in the year 303 for defying the Emperor Diocletian.

His cult began during the eleventh century. St. George is said to have appeared at the Siege of Antioch in 1089 and helped the Crusaders to turn the tide. The story of this gallant and handsome young cavalry officer seems to have caught the imagination of troubadours and fighting men all over Europe. They carried back his cult to their various homelands together with the spices and sugar which were to change the whole character of diet in Europe. By the fourteenth century, George had become the patron saint of Christian cavalry and of soldiers in general.

England already had a patron saint, Edward the Confessor. However, King Edward III was devoted to St. George. On 23rd April 1349 he created the highest order of English chivalry, the Order of the Garter, under the patronage of St. George to whom he dedicated the Order's chapel at Windsor. In the same year the King instituted the 'Poor Knights of Windsor' or Military Knights, as they are now called. His idea was to provide an honourable asylum and subsistence for old soldiers 'decayed in wars and suchlike service of the realm'. Although disciplined, the Knights must have fed well. At least, all the scraps from their table were given to the poor, together with the dishes, plates and tablecloths. (This was a standard way to hand out largesse after a feast in mediaeval times, and meant a free-for-all riot as soon as the gates were opened.)

Most of us know the traditional English recipe which instructs the cook to fry Poor Knights a nice pale brown in a hot pan! It sounds sheer cannibalism, unless you know that it is just bread slices fried in butter, sprinkled with sugar and cinnamon—a dessert for which we have recipes dating back to the year 1400. However, the recipe is no more exclusively English than St. George. The dish is known by the same name in Scandinavia, Germany and especially Vienna. Sweden also introduced a version called Rich Knights where almonds are added to the egg batter in which the bread is fried. In Germany they soak their Knights in red wine, spread them with fresh crushed strawberries and then with meringue. Far away in Argentina the Knights were obviously not so poor either as the version there is steeped in port, simmered in the oven after frying and then served with sweet whipped cream.

SHAKESPEARE'S BIRTHDAY

The old drinks Sack and Malmsey are a feature at the Shakespeare birthday dinner celebrated at Stratford upon Avon. In Shakespeare's day both were new and fashionable; perhaps that is why he mentioned them frequently in his plays.

Ever since Crusader times the English had had a taste for the sweet wines of Southern Europe. One of these was Malmsey, as they called the Malvoisie wine from Greece. It became so popular that around 1420 the sweet wine grapes had been specially planted by Portuguese colonists on the island of Madeira together with Sicilian sugar cane. As a result, Madeira Malmsey was one of England's favourite drinks throughout the fifteenth and sixteenth centuries. Andrew Boorde, writing in 1542, described it as 'a hot wine . . . not good to drink with meat, but after meat with oysters,

Milk featured in many May Day feasts.

Milkmaids' May Dance in London—note the silver garlands.

with salads, with fruit'.

In the early sixteenth century the wine makers of southern Spain, particularly around Jerez, were quick to offer British importers special terms for their dry amber Sack. But it was not sweet enough for the Elizabethans who added to it that other great Crusader import, sugar.

MAY DAY

Almost every village in Britain used to celebrate the start of the Celtic summer with its own local rituals. May Day was a phallic pagan festival and a time when witches were powerful. Even in 1870 a good Christian parson like Francis Kilvert smilingly thought that he should protect his home against them with rowan branches. But in general May Eve and May Day were cheerful times, and their rituals were happy ones of gathering flowers, making garlands, dancing and sports.

Naturally food featured in these rituals too. Woodland wanderers gathering May boughs, or lasses who got up at dawn to wash their faces in May dew needed sustenance. Still more did the energetic Maypole dancers or the boys and girls who went from farm to farm carrying the May Garland. In *The Diary of a Farmer's Wife* Anne Hughes of Herefordshire records how she made May Cakes on 30th April 1796 for 'whoever might cum amaying'. These cakes were made of buttercrust pastry 'cut in little rounds', filled with a 'messe' of finely chopped meat, apple, onion, lemon thyme, rosemary and seasoning. Small custard tarts with ground almonds, currant and peel are recorded as traditional May Day Cakes in Berwick in Northumberland. In Cornwall young people went around the farms blowing horns to announce summer's return and claiming junket and cream for breakfast as well as cake.

Milk featured in May Day feasts in several other areas. In Northumberland, they had syllabub 'made from the warm milk from the cow, sweet cake and wine', and in the Black Country, colliers and ironworkers in the last century used to drink a whey drink made of rum and milk. An unusual custom still goes on at Randwick in Gloucestershire. Here three local cheeses are garlanded and carried through the village on May morning. These cheeses are bowled round the church three times and then taken to the village green where they are cut up and handed to parishioners.

In London, milkmaids and dairymaids carried special silver garlands and danced outside the houses of their customers.

April 22

April 29

April 23
St. George
Shakespeare's Birthday

April 30

April 24

May 1
SS. Philip and James

April 25
St. Mark

May 2

April 26

May 3

April 27

May 4

April 28

May 5

ROGATIONTIDE

Rogationtide consists of Rogation Sunday on the fifth Sunday after Easter and the three following days leading up to Ascension Day. These were days of penitence and abstinence, and at the same time God's blessing was sought on the new green crops, especially to keep them free from blight. The Major Rogation, which is probably the oldest, now falls outside Rogationtide itself as a rule, on 25th April.

Since mediaeval people were practical, the practice grew up of Beating the Bounds of the parish at the same time as invoking God's blessing on the crops. This ritual was a way of making the then illiterate parishioners remember where the boundaries lay, without recourse to mysterious maps. Wherever the boundary was obscure or took a sharp turn, a boundary stone was set up. Clergy and parishioners processed from stone to stone, and at each one the boys were bumped on the stone, beaten with peeled wands over it, or else ducked in a nearby ditch to remind them forcibly of just where it lay. The less penitential parishioners refreshed themselves liberally along the route on the bread and ale provided by the parish.

In time, instead of beating the boys, the boys themselves beat the stones with wands or staves. In this form, the ritual still takes place in a number of parishes such as St. Michael-in-the-Northgate in Oxford. Here, the boundary stone lies in the Roebuck Inn, where the landlord provides cheer in much the old style. The last stop is Lincoln College where the company get a traditional Ploughman's-Lunch-style meal of bread, cheese, salad and spring onions with potent Ivy Beer (flavoured with steeped Ground Ivy), possibly dating back to the old mediaeval herb ales.

In villages on the coast, the main produce was and still is fish, not corn. At Brixham on Rogation Sunday a service is still held at the harbour to seek God's blessing on the fishermen and the harvest of the sea.

A RADISH FEAST

A fascinating spring feast recorded for this book by two local Women's Institute members used to be held on 12th May each year at Levens Hall, a fine Tudor mansion in Westmorland. The owner, one Colonel James Graham, founded the Radish Feast around 1700, ostensibly to mark the beating of the bounds of lands belonging to him within the parish of Milnthorpe. In fact, Colonel Graham felt insulted because the owner of the neighbouring mansion Dallam Tower entertained the Mayor of Kendal at the opening of Milnthorpe Fair.

Colonel Graham's Feast was an all-male affair. Four men worked for a full day cleaning barrowloads of radishes, all grown in the gardens of Levens Hall. These were eaten with haverbread (North Country thin oatcakes) or bread and butter. The repast was washed down with a potent brown ale called Morocco Beer, which was said to be kept for twenty-one years before being tapped. The recipe was secret, but was alleged to contain meat as well as the more usual malt and hops. It was oily in consistency and deceptively mild in flavour, a trap for the unwary since it had a knock-out effect. The Levens Hall version threw a heavy crust which effectively sealed the liquor from the air until the last drop was broached, so it kept its strength to the end.

The Radish Feast ceased when a strictly teetotal lady, Mrs. Mary Howard, became owner of the Hall in the 1870's. But luckily by that time, the ill-will between the owners of the two mansions was a thing of the past.

A LOVE FEAST

The Wicken Love Feast originated not in a quarrel, but the reverse. In 1587, after years of bitter feuding, the parishes of Wykeham and Wykedyke in Northamptonshire were 'unighted' as a local lady wrote in 1810, into one parish called Wicken. The happy event was at first celebrated by an ox-roasting on Ascension Day, but later took the form she described, as follows:

After a morning service 'the 100 psalm is sung under an Elem Tree near the Parsonage where the Rector has given cake and ail to all the Parish that assembled or came to it as a remembrance . . . The quantities of ail flower and ingredients is spessified.'

Even the 'spessified' ingredients are given in this record. For any enthusiastic home baker who wants to initiate a similar feast they were: "Three Bushels of Wheat to be made into cakes with six pounds of Butter, six pounds of Currants, a pound of Carraway Seeds with as many cloves and allspice as will make up one shillingsworth in the whole. Sixteen cakes of the largest sort to weigh six pounds each into the oven. All the remaining Flour to be made into cakes to weigh four pounds and a half into the oven'. These cakes were at that time probably loaves of yeasted spiced currant bread wetted with ale 'barm', but in modern times conventional seed cake has been substituted.

Love Feasts, rather like peace meetings, were common among early nonconformist sects. One such survives at Alport in Derbyshire, which dates back to the time when nonconformists had to meet in secret. Each member of the congregation, we are told, receives a small piece of fruit cake, and a Loving Cup of water is shared. Such a Love Feast could make a pleasant form of children's service, introducing them to the ancient idea of sharing food as a sacrament.

May 6

May 13

May 7

May 14

May 8

May 15

May 9

May 16

May 10

May 17

May 11

May 18

May 12

May 19

WHITSUNTIDE

Sports and Cheese

Gloucestershire cheeses were famous for their rich golden beauty and flavour long before cheeses actually had their own distinctive names. For more than four hundred years a cheerful cheese-rolling race has taken place every Whit Monday (nowadays on Spring Bank Holiday) on Cooper's Hill. It commemorates an ancient custom whereby villagers used to gather in order to assert their right to graze livestock on the local common land.

There was however rather more to cheese-rolling than this. Long ago the cheeses were wreathed in flaming brushwood. This custom seems to derive from the ancient practice of rolling fiery spherical objects around in symbolic celebration of the return of the summer sun. Perhaps we can thus claim a living link between Gloucester cheese and the primitive sacrifice of the land's richest produce by the old pagan sun-worshippers.

Unbroken even in wartime, the Cooper's Hill celebration has changed little with time. Only stalwart lads compete, because the rough one-in-three gradient is slippery, and the Race is more like a headlong rush, with risk to knees and ankles if no more. At the count the Starter releases the cheese and then the competitors go bounding down the slope. The contestants try to overtake the cheese before it reaches the bottom of the hill, but success is rare, since it always bounces this way and that at great speed. In any case, whoever reaches the bottom first is the winner who keeps the cheese, while the runners-up get small money prizes.

Another, less violent Gloucestershire event is the Scramble at St. Briavels. Bread and cheese is still distributed to all villagers after Evensong on Whit Sunday. At first the distribution took place from the church pulpit, but later it was settled that baskets should be emptied from the top of a high wall near the church, and the people below should scramble for the pieces of bread and cheese thrown to them. In fact scrambling is another ancient group custom. As at Cooper's Hill, the St. Briavels event protects the villagers' right to graze cattle, and also to cut timber in nearby Hudnall's Wood.

Revels and Ales

Whitsuntide stands out as the Christian year's most cheerful season, second only to Christmas. From mediaeval times, revels, with their sports and fun were the order of the day. Mystery and miracle plays were performed by town guilds or travelling mummers. At Liskeard in Cornwall publicans organized gymnastic displays, wrestling, sack races and donkey racing. Elsewhere the sports included skittles, boxing, football, and climbing a greasy pole for a ham or leg of mutton set on top. Staid housewives ran races for a gown or a Sunday joint, men wrestled for hats and silver spoons. Citizens used to place small trees outside their houses to show they could sell ale without a licence for the duration of the Revel, while sweets of almonds, sugar and spices, and gingerbread nuts or buttons were sold from stalls for lads to give girls.

Church Ales were another Whitsun feature in many parishes. An Ale was a group fund-raising effort as well as a chance to have a good time. In most parishes there was a Church House, where cooking utensils were kept. Here housewives made merry and gave their services as cooks, while young people danced and

played darts. As a rule a Lord and Lady of the Ale were elected to run the festivities, often with Officers who collected money or provisions to make the Ale a success.

The Woodstock Ale in Oxfordshire took place every seven years. The Lord and Lady went around the town bearing a huge cake, which people tasted for a small payment. Small currant Whit Cakes were also sold to raise funds for parish needs. Everyone paid cheerfully for their cakes as they drank freely, danced and sang round a maypole or watched the Morris Dancers.

Certain foods were always associated with Whitsun. Seasonal foods such as cheesecakes, baked custards, roast veal and gooseberry pies were customary. At London's Greenwich Fair there were stewed prunes, plum cakes and bottled ale as well as vast quantities of cheesecakes and custards. There were many kinds of Whitsun cakes too. Yorkshire and Durham folk ate cheesecakes, while in Lancashire they ate sugar-glazed muffins called Top Cakes. In fact the variety of food is best summed up in this verse, recorded in 1899:

> *Each different county boasts a diff'rent taste,*
> *And owes its fame to pudding and to paste;*
> *Squab pie in Cornwall only, can they make;*
> *In Norfolk dumplings, and in Salop, cake.*
> *But Oxford now from all shall bear the prize,*
> *Fam'd, as for sausages, for mutton pies.*

Ram Roastings

Ram roastings took place at a number of Devon villages. Probably associated with ancient pagan sacrifices, the only survival is at Kingsteignton.

Left: Dancing at Whitsuntide.
Right: Another Whitsun event, The Scouring of the White Horse on the Berkshire Downs.

The Woodstock Ale in Blenheim Park.

It is said that in early British times the local stream dried up. When people prayed to their gods water at once sprang from the land of an estate later called Rydon, and so a sacrificial lamb has been offered yearly thereafter as a thanksgiving.

The ceremonies used to extend over Whit Monday and Tuesday. On the first day the living lamb, chosen as the finest from the local flocks, was taken through the village on a flower-decked waggon. Next day it was killed, the carcass was paraded and then roasted. Slices of the hot meat were and are said to bring good luck. Sports and games go on during the roasting, and nowadays slices are distributed by ballot, as so many people attend the event.

May 20

May 21

May 22

May 23

May 24

May 25

May 26
St. Augustine

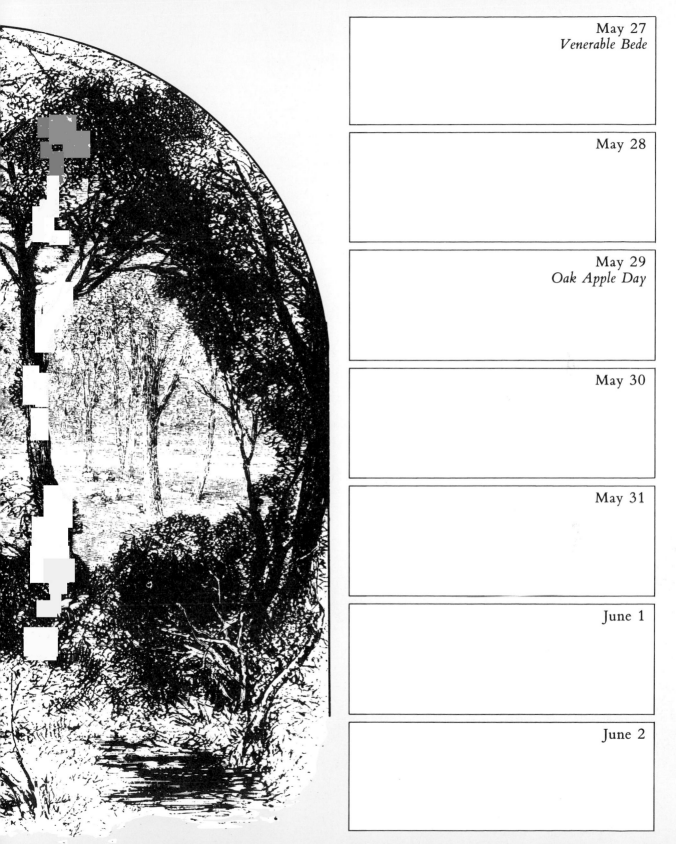

May 27
Venerable Bede

May 28

May 29
Oak Apple Day

May 30

May 31

June 1

June 2

THREE BAGS FULL

Sheep shearing took place at about the same time as haymaking. It was often a communal task, made pleasant by entertaining the friends and neighbours who came to help, as Thomas Tusser described in the sixteenth century. Afterwards, the shepherd would inspect every beast, clean it up and treat it for fly-blow, maggots or scratches. Finally, the women or sometimes the shearers themselves would clean, fold and bind the fleeces, ready for packing in great heavy sacks.

All this was hard work, with only short breaks. There was a brief rest at dinner-time, and usually one in the afternoon with mugs of tea or ale and sweet bread (in Devon, splits or cut-rounds) with butter or cream. At the end, there would be a merry supper for all. To eat there might be a joint of beef, pigeon or rook pies, syllabubs or junket and new-made cheese. There was also a big spicy Shearing Cake and plenty of specially brewed Shearing Ale. Then the youngsters danced to the shepherds' pipes and the 'old'uns' would sing, and the ale would go round until well into the night.

LAMB ALES

Lamb Ales were a Trinity Monday custom in Oxfordshire. The Kirtlington Ale opened with the choice of a local lad to be Lord in charge of the festivities. His first task was to select a modest, respectable and pretty girl as his Lady. Both were paid a small sum. For the first three days they visited with a retinue every point in the parish, sporting pink and blue emblems, the Dashwood family colours, and followed by the local Morris Dancers. The procession was headed by a fine lamb carried shoulder-high. This sacrificial beast was slaughtered and cooked on the third day, and 'lucky' lamb pies were then made with the meat and shared out. The head, left whole with its wool on, went into a special pie, which was then sold as a potent charm for good fortune.

The Kirtlington Lamb Ale was revived in 1981, principally as a Morris Dance festival, but with a traditional dance by Kirtlington maidens around the Lady of the Lamb. There is a procession to the church, during which the Lady is escorted by a Lord, who is one of the Morris Dancers. She carries a lamb, while two Morris men carry the traditional Forest Feathers, and two maidens carry maces with lamb pies on top. The whole occasion is a picturesque festival for participants and spectators alike.

HAY HARVEST

Fragrant hay provided the first harvest of the year. In most of England mowing traditionally began by St. Barnabas Day. Hay was a highly valuable crop. Unlike cattle which could be fed on straw, heavy shire-type horses and the vastly increased flocks of sheep bred for the wool trade from Tudor times needed hay. Cowman and shepherd tried to hoard hay for their breeding stock too.

Everyone in the villages took part in haymaking, even the doctor and the parson. Until the days of motorised transport the only way to get round a scattered practice or parish was by pony and trap or on horseback. Many, if not most, parsons combined their spiritual duties with the earthly occupation of farming their glebe lands in order to provide their families with milk and bacon, and their cows, pigs and horses with hay or oats.

Haymaking was performed with less ceremony than cutting the corn. Mowing came first, with scythes, or later by machine. Hand mowers usually worked through the heat of the day, only refreshing themselves with a draught of ale brought along by a small boy from time to time, and with a short noon break for bread and cheese, more ale and a quick nap. In Cumberland they had a haytime and harvest drink made of oatmeal, sugar and lemon, described as 'a real slakin' drink'. Supper would be almost the same as the noonday snack: bread, cheese, baby onions and more ale.

Tossing and making the hay followed, and now the women and children played a major part. The swathes of grass were tossed and turned over to dry thoroughly. Lunch was a picnic in the field with milk, buttermilk or lemonade for girls and youngsters, and again with simple bread and cheese. The dry grass then had to be gathered and taken back to the yard, where it was bedded, stacked in ricks and thatched. This thirsty work demanded refreshment with 'small' beer at frequent intervals.

Being less formal haymaking ended, not with a full-scale supper like the corn harvest, but with a slap-up tea to which everyone came in their Sunday best. Usually it started after milking. Foaming fresh milk would be the lot of lucky children, although their elders had tea or a stronger brew. There would be new-baked bread, farm butter and a fine solid cake as well as ham and a salad. Then after tea, there would be games and dancing well into the evening.

Sheep-shearing and haymaking took place around the same time.

June 3

June 4

June 5

June 6

June 7

June 8

June 9

June 10

June 11
St. Barnabas

June 12

June 13

June 14

June 15

June 16

MIDSUMMER

Bonfires and Magic

Since Christian times the Church has equated the pagan Midsummer or summer solstice fire rituals with the feast of St. John the Baptist. Midsummer bonfires were customary in many parts of the country until well into this century, and some have been revived recently in Cornwall. In pagan times fires were lit on the hill tops to strengthen the sun, and until quite recently were accompanied by flaming tar barrels hoisted on poles, flaming wheels rolling down hillsides and torchlight processions.

Many of these fire rituals were similar to those which Celtic peoples performed in May. They were all designed to bring fertility and well-being to men, as well as to their crops and cattle—in other words their food. Dancing sunwise round the fire and leaping through it, and driving cattle through the ashes or smoke were also purifying and protective rituals against witches. Witches were said to be abroad and potent at this time, so stinking smoke from burning bones was sometimes used to keep them at bay.

Herbs and plants were used in plenty as protection at Midsummer. Green birch, fennel, St. John's Wort and rue were all guardian charms. Rowan could be plaited in cows' tails or tucked in one's pocket if travelling. Seeds were magical. Fern seed gave both protection against witches and the gift of invisibility. Midsummer was also a good time for marriage divining (like Hallowe'en in Scotland). If a girl scattered hemp seed around the churchyard at midnight on Midsummer Eve, her future husband would appear raking or mowing the seed. Anne Hughes recorded hearing her servant-girl get up at midnight in 1796 to scatter hemp seed where the lad she fancied would walk, and remembered doing the same herself.

Midsummer Tithes

Midsummer was one of the customary times for paying tithes. A tithe was one tenth of the produce of the land or its cash equivalent, which was paid by farmers to the parish priest or rector. Strictly speaking, the paying of tithes is not a folk custom, but the curious forms which it took became an extraordinary patchwork with long-forgotten origins only recorded in local memories.

We get a fascinating account of one set of Midsummer Tithes in *The History of Myddle* by Richard Gough, written between 1700 and 1702 about a Shropshire village. Some of the tithes had been commuted into straight cash payments, but the rest were a complex pattern of payments in kind, which must have made for chaos in the rectory fowl yard and fold yard. If a parishioner had seven lambs, pigs or geese, the rector got one, but was paid three halfpence for the three short of ten, but if there were fewer than seven, he got a halfpenny in lieu of each. This meant that if a parishioner had for example fifteen geese, the rector got a goose and two and a half pence. A farmer owning all three kinds of livestock would choose two of the three to be handed over, and the recipient chose the third. But if any had been sold before tithe time, the recipient chose from the unsold ones only, and the owner of any sheep sold in the wool had to pay a cash sum for each month that he had 'possessed' the wool since the last shearing time.

Often in small parishes the reckoning or audit of the tithes was a group gathering of the debtor farmers with the parson, and it was usual for him to give them a Tithe Dinner afterwards. Thus the eighteenth century diarist Parson Woodforde had twenty-two tithe payers to a dinner at his December audit in 1786. He fed them on salt fish, a leg of mutton boiled with capers, boiled and roast beef, and a choice of plain and plum puddings. To drink they had between them six bottles of rum made into punch, seven bottles of wine, and a 'great quantity' of strong beer.

Peace and Good Neighbourhood

At Kidderminster in Worcestershire a dinner is held every Midsummer Eve, when a Chairman offers to settle any disputes between the inhabitants of Church Street, and then offers a toast to Peace and Good Neighbourhood. This special neighbourly custom is the result of two bequests. The first was made in the fifteenth century by an unknown spinster, who left forty shillings to be put out to interest to provide 'farthing loaves' for the people of the street, and to enable all male inhabitants to be friendly and to compose any differences. A fine idea in an age when few people went more than a few miles from home in a lifetime, and neighbours made up one's sole community. This bequest was added to three hundred years later when John Brecknell left £150 on his death in 1778 to provide plum cakes as well as pipes, tobacco and ale for the men at the midsummer assembly. The custom died out during the war, but was revived in 1951. It would be pleasant if the street parties which now take place on special occasions in some of our cities could develop into this kind of get-together dinner.

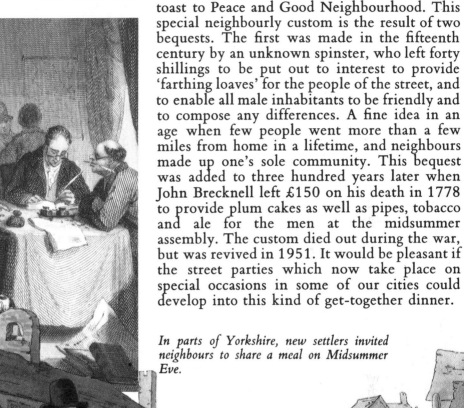

In parts of Yorkshire, new settlers invited neighbours to share a meal on Midsummer Eve.

June 17
St. Alban

June 24
St. John the Baptist

June 18

June 25

June 19

June 26

June 20

June 27

June 21

June 28

June 22

June 29
St. Peter

June 23

June 30

Vauxhall Gardens, showing the Long Walk and company at supper, c. 1750.

SUMMER FARE

Strawberries are one of our oldest native plants, and still a treat in spite of mass production. Yet they hardly feature at all in our folklore. The strawberry events that we celebrate are historically modern happenings.

The reason for this may be that classical and mediaeval doctors had a low opinion of the health value of fruit. This seems foolish to us, but it was science to them. It is interesting because it helps to explain some of the folktales that have grown up about plants. Here is a piece about strawberries from John Russell's *Boke of Nurture*, written about 1450:

> *Bewar at eve of crayme of cowe and also*
> *of the goote . . . , of strawberies and*
> *hurtilberyes with the cold ioncate (cream*
> *junket with rose water and sugar) . . .*
> *for these may marre many a man chan-*
> *gynge*
> *his estate (making him feel ill) . . .*
> *(unless he has) after hard chese (and)*
> *wafurs with wyne ypocrate (sweet ginger*
> *wine).*

In other words, don't eat strawberries and cream before you go to bed, because it will be lowering unless you eat hard cheese and wafers afterwards.

Standard medical thinking at that time was still influenced by ancient Greek ideas on diet. It was held that every food had a Quality gained from two out of the four elements: air was dry, water was moist, fire was hot and earth was cold. Food was only good for you if its Quality suited your own. Derived from this theory, people thought that too much fruit could cause 'putrid' fevers in reaction against its cold, moist Quality. It should therefore only be eaten sparingly, if at all. Certainly one should not eat fruit at night, because it was also sexually lowering. However, if hard cheese, which had a hot dry Quality were eaten afterwards, it would counteract this unfortunate consequence. Hard cheese also made a layer or seal over the wine in one's stomach, and thus stopped it rising to the brain—or that was the hopeful idea.

56

It is not hard to see how the ban on fruit came about. In the past people had little idea of hygiene, and in summer when flies bred freely on farmyard dunghills and in open street drains, fevers, diarrhoea and dysentry were rife. It was easy, and sometimes right, to blame it all on too much unwashed fruit.

Right up to the beginning of the nineteenth century, fruit was only thought good for you if it was candied or boiled to a pulp as a pie filling, or was used for the then fashionable homemade fruit wines and spirits.

Not all fresh fruit was shunned. Wild cherries and strawberries were always popular, as a change. For instance, Samuel Pepys in the 1660's used to take his wife Elizabeth to Vauxhall Gardens to pick wild cherries. In the early nineteenth century, Lady Caroline Lamb took a strawberry-seller with her when she organised (and cooked) a picnic meal there.

Later on, Vauxhall, was famous for its myriad lights, concerts and fireworks, and also for other foods besides fruit. Royalty came to enjoy its famous paper-thin slices of ham. By contrast, the apprentices and their girls, and the river taximen could get solid meat pies, sausages or pickled oysters from the pie shops and booths along the river bank. It was not wise to sniff them too closely. For five hundred years royal edicts had been published regularly to discipline dishonest cooks and pie-makers, but without the slightest success.

Most people had drunk enough by the time they left Foxhall not to notice any other queasiness. The drinks were many and varied. Citron Wine was a favourite strongly alcoholic lemonade, and Vauxhall Nectar was another popular powerful brew. The menu in 1760 included five types of wine at around six shillings a bottle. There was Champagne at eight shillings a bottle or cheaper wine at two shillings. Cider cost one shilling, and a quart of light beer fourpence. Made-up drinks such as Nectar or Hippocras cost more. Sir Roger de Coverley on a visit to Vauxhall in 1711 was accosted by a buxom, masked young woman who invited him to buy her a drink of this sweet ginger wine. Having replied with some well-chosen words, the knight escaped to go (literally) for a Burton.

Branded ales were all the rage in those days. They were a good deal more wholesome than the cheap brews which contained isin-glass, chalk and treacle, and which were sold by the glass in the South of England. Common brewers heavily adulterated their beers and ales as well as their wines, often with most undesirable substances. Tobacco for instance was used as colouring and copperas (vitriol) was added to give beer a head. The passing trade, whether sightseer or traveller, was fair game, as it had always been.

Strawberries, scarlet strawberries, 1795.

July 1

July 2

July 3

July 4

July 5

58

July 6

July 7

July 8

July 9

July 10

July 11

July 12

July 13

July 14

July 15
St. Swithun

DRINKING MEMORIES

Ale drinking ceremonies are as old as ale. But more unusual, and once more serious, survivals are connected with old mediaeval administration. The Courts Leet and Baron, which originally dealt with manorial rights, still appoint officials to tour the town of Ashburton in Devon during July. Their job is to taste the ale at all the inns, and to issue an evergreen branch or sprig to those which meet their standards. The bakers' bread is also weighed to make sure that it conforms to the law, which used to fix a price for each type of bread by weight. At Andover in Hampshire an Ale Taster has been elected annually ever since the reign of Queen Elizabeth I.

A more abstemious Tudor drinking assessment is still carried out annually at Plymouth on the nearest Saturday to 14th July. We usually think of Sir Francis Drake as a great admiral and explorer, rather than a sober civic-minded citizen. But after 1588 he set to work to create a water supply for the city of Plymouth, and ever since 1603 it has been inspected annually.

Today the Lord Mayor leads a procession to the Corporation reservoir. Each guest in turn tastes the reservoir water from a silver goblet, with the words, 'To the pious memory of Sir Francis Drake'. The guests then drink from a second goblet, repeating, 'May the descendants of him who brought water never want for wine.'

ST JAMES'S SHELLS

St. James the Great has a direct connection with food in both ancient and modern folklore. The ancient and lasting one is his emblem, a scallop shell, which used to be worn by pilgrims who visited his shrine at Compostella in Spain. Such a pilgrim in his broad shovel hat and cloak with his staff and badge has been immortalized in the poem by Sir Walter Raleigh, which begins 'Give me my scallop shell of quiet'.

We do not know how or why the slum children of London picked up the idea of building copies of St. James's shrine in shells. They were certainly doing it from the mid-eighteenth century up until the Second World War. Scallop shells were used in earlier days,

Oyster Day: 'Please Remember the Grotto'.

but throughout Victorian times oysters sold from stalls and booths were a common food, even for the desperately poor, as Charles Dickens testifys in *The Pickwick Papers*. So even the poorest child could get oyster shells to construct a grotto, which was decorated with brightly coloured bits of broken china and flowering weeds, usually with a small space inside for a lighted candle end. The child would then wait, cap in hand, and beg for pennies 'for the Grotto' from passers-by.

HORN FAIR

The Horn Fair held at Ebernoe in Sussex on St. James's Day may go back to a time when the horns were those of a wild beast killed by a village round-up, the prized head being the trophy of the bravest. Horns originally had many magical uses—for expelling witches, ghosts and illnesses, for new moon and sunset ceremonies, as well as for protecting trees, crops and the home from evil spirits. Because of their crescent shape, horns were associated with all forms of moon magic.

The Fair now has only one small link with these magical properties. A horned sheep is roasted in a pit near the local cricket ground, and the meat is basted by the visitors for 'luck'. The Ebernoe cricket team meanwhile play another team. Afterwards the teams have a roast mutton lunch, and the highest scoring batsman gets the horns—perhaps with a few gibes about married life.

PIGS & PLUM PUDDINGS

A quite different feast, both communal and comic, took place at Newbury in Berkshire on the first Monday after St. Anne's Day. Its ceremonies centred on the election of a Mock Mayor, and Hone's *Every Day Book* of 1838 describes how 'At the Bull and Dog Inn a ceremony of electing the 'Mayor of Bartlemas' takes place and a dinner is prepared at the aforesaid inn, the principal dishes being bacon and beans, when the feast is called the Bacon and Bean Feast. During the day there is a Mayoral Procession, in which a cabbage stalk on a pole is conspicuous and serves as the Mace'.

The feast did have one serious point to make. It promoted, even without meaning to, a product of which Berkshire people were rightly proud. Berkshire pigs are still renowned as self-reliant, common-sensical, sturdy creatures, well able to forage for themselves. Their flesh is firm, making compact bacon and ham joints, and for this reason pork was a characteristic Berkshire dish, even in the summer heat.

Another feature of most Berkshire summer feasts was plum pudding. At Radley, for instance, all August occasions were marked by the eating of plum puddings and the drinking of quantities of ginger beer. A warm way to take one's pleasure!

A SALMON FEAST

Tweedmouth in Northumberland used to be one of the main centres of the salmon industry. Although its market has long lapsed, the Crowning of the Salmon Queen ceremonies were revived in 1945, and take place during the last two weeks in July. Before the crowning ceremony the Queen crosses the River Tweed in the traditional Salmon Cable boat. There is a church service and the Queen lays a wreath at the War Memorial. After the crowning there is a Salmon Supper attended by the Queen and local dignitaries.

Supervising weights and measures.

July 16

July 17

July 18

July 19

July 20

July 21

July 22

July 23

July 24

July 25
St. James

July 26
St. Anne

July 27

July 28

July 29

RUSHES & RUSHBEARING

The hall of a mediaeval castle usually had a stone-flagged floor, which was covered by loose, sometimes scented rushes, and in summer and autumn by herbs and flowers as well. When crushed underfoot they scented the whole room. The rich had their food and their washing water perfumed as well, and until the eighteenth century, long after rushes had gone out, they strewed fragrant herbs on their fires. Popular strewing herbs included basil, balm, costmary, fennel, hops lavender, marjoram, pennyroyal, roses, sage and tansy.

Churches also had rushes or sometimes hay strewn on their stone or beaten earth floors. Unlike those of the castle hall, church rushes were usually only replaced once a year, as a rule in the first week in August, and the whole

Laying rushes in the Presence Chamber, Hardwick Hall.

parish would take part. There was a procession, perhaps around the parish bounds, in which girls and boys carried wreaths and banners of rushes and flowers. Musicians and dancers might accompany the cartloads of rushes and church bells would ring. Quite a number of churches in the North Country and Midlands still had an annual Rushbearing ceremony during the nineteenth century, but the only two well-known ones to survive are at Ambleside and Grasmere, both in Westmorland.

The Ambleside Rushbearing used to take place on the Saturday nearest St. Anne's Day, but is now held on the first Saturday in July. It is an elaborate ritual. The rushes to be presented to the church are made up on wooden bearings into many shapes: the Harp of David leads the procession, followed by the church-wardens' Staves, the Crown and the World (a new introduction). They are intricately decorated with mosses, rushes and flowers, and are

A Lancashire rushbearing at Failsworth.

too heavy for children to carry, but between three and four hundred children follow with their own smaller bearings. The procession stops in the market place to sing the Rushbearers' Hymn, composed by the Vicar of Ambleside early last century. The bearings are then taken to the church for the Rushbearing Service, and as they leave the children are all given gingerbread. Sports are held on the following Monday.

The Grasmere Rushbearing is considerably older. It takes place on the Saturday nearest to St. Oswald's Day, and William Wordsworth recorded the event in one of his poems. Nearly every child in the village carries a bearing or a basket of rushes and flowers. The procession, which is accompanied by the village band playing the ancient Rushbearing tune, includes the six Rush Maidens carrying the Rush Sheet, a maypole and several large elaborate bearings.

Meanwhile, the church has been strewn with rushes one inch deep. After the service the children receive the traditional piece of gingerbread made by the village baker, and stamped with the mark of St. Oswald. This soft type of gingerbread is not the same as the Grasmere Gingerbread made from a secret recipe and sold in the village.

LAMMAS

Lammas celebrated a moment heavy with meaning for early Christian men. This was when the first bread was made from the new season's corn and then offered to the Church. The word is said to come from 'loaf-mass' (Saxon: hlaefmas), the new bread being conse-crated during the service of the mass. Lammas seems to go back to the Celtic fertility festival called the Lugnasad, which took place on 1st August, exactly nine months before the feast of Beltane marking the start of summer. The festival celebrated the symbolic marriage of the earth-mother goddess, and earthly marriages were arranged then. Games were played and several fairs were held. The Lammas Fair in Exeter was revived in 1939, and the famous Ripon Fair continues today. Wilfra Cakes, named after St. Wilfrid of Ripon and consisting of apple and cheese, are still made for the feast. Large plates of these used to be placed inside the doors of houses for passers-by to help themselves.

PIE PLENTY

Although the serious business of getting in the corn harvest kept most farmers fully occupied in pre-mechanized England early in August, there was time for celebrations in some places. The harvesting of the black cherry crop was marked by festivals in Buckinghamshire and in the Chiltern villages of Hertfordshire. In Hampshire Merrie Sundays were a feature of the cherry season.

In some places the first Sunday in July was known as Gooseberry Pie Sunday. A more modern occasion is the Old Gooseberry Show held at Egton Bridge in North Yorkshire on the first Tuesday in August. All the berries competing are mammoths, with royal and lordly names such as Prince Charles, Princess Royal and Lord Derby, and even, although now rare, a yellow smooth berry called Thatcher. The record heavy berry in this century was exhibited in 1978, and weighed 2.6 ounces. Bilberries also feature in North Yorkshire, where they are made into pies and served with cream early in July, while at Lickey in Worcestershire they used to hold a Bilberry Wake.

The main feature of the carnival day at Denby Dale near Barnsley in South Yorkshire, sometimes held on the first Monday in August, has been on six occasions a Two-Ton Pie. This huge pie was first made to celebrate the recovery of King George III from an illness in 1788. It consists of mixed meat and potato. One pie, which may not have been the largest, is reputed to have contained 1492 pounds of meat meat in a crust made with 1120 pounds of flour.

July 30	August 6
July 31	August 7
August 1 *Lammas*	August 8
August 2	August 9
August 3	August 10 *St. Lawrence*
August 4	August 11
August 5 *St. Oswald*	August 12

GREAT ENGLISH FAIRS

Fairs grew up in ancient times, long before there were shops or even weekly markets. Warring tribes or rival groups had to find a time and place of amnesty so that they could celebrate religious festivals or trade in safety. The Church took over and adapted the great pagan festivals and their fairs with them. Although some old bartering fairs became specialized seasonal fairs, dealing in horses, cattle or other livestock, or produce such as apples and cheese, most church-based and some trading fairs sold anything and everything, so that a mediaeval housewife could stock up once a year with basic supplies and household goods, rather like going to the sales.

She might not get bargains from the hard-headed hucksters, but she had some protection against being swindled, because every proper fair operated under a Charter. Whoever had bought or been granted the Charter had the right and the duty to regulate the running of the fair. He (or she) might take over a town entirely, and appoint, as the Bishop of Winchester did, his own law officers, inspectors of goods, and justices who would impose fines or forfeitures. Courts were held as well. Furthermore, no-one might sell goods locally except at the fair after paying the proper tolls and customs duty. Holding the Charter of a big fair was like owning a gold mine.

The great national fairs of Winchester and St. Ives were both church-owned in mediaeval times. The stream of devout visitors who prayed and purchased alternately brought immense wealth. Winchester's fair started on the feast of St. Giles, and the Abbot of Ramsey Abbey in Huntingdonshire, which owned the shrine of St. Ive, ran his fair. A trading fair licensed by Royal Charter was the Exeter Lammas Fair, and the nearby Honiton Fair was originally granted to the Lady of the Manor.

Sturbridge Fair

Sturbridge (Stourbridge) Fair in Cambridgeshire was the greatest of the national fairs. No other English fair could compete with it in its heyday. For three weeks, from 24th August each year, one could buy almost anything, wholesale or retail, at Sturbridge. There were Italian silks, velvet and glass, Flemish linens,

Entertainment at a country fair.

A booth at Stourbridge Fair.

Gascon, Spanish and Mediterranean wines. There were furs, amber and precious stones from Moscow, Cornish tin, Derbyshire lead, Sussex iron, wool—and food.

Under Queen Elizabeth I the town of Cambridge got the right to control the fair, while the university got the right to regulate the sale of bread, wine, ale and beer, along with the right to search for and punish harlots and vagabonds. Perhaps the most outstanding character was the Lord of the Taps who sampled the ale in a splendid red coat decorated with taps—real ones. But the biggest show was the opening procession and proclamation of the fair on 24th August. Once the fair was proclaimed open, there followed a banquet at which fresh herrings were always the chief dish.

Other foods were associated with Sturbridge Fair. There was roast goose, which came into season just in time, and roast and boiled pork were also enjoyed. Other specialities were large oysters from King's Lynn, walnuts and gingerbread. Many tons of cheese were sold at the cheese booths. Dealers came from Cheshire and Wiltshire, and farmers from Norfolk and Suffolk sold large quantities of Cottenham and cream cheese.

Daniel Defoe described how overnight a miniature London was set up at Sturbridge, with coffee-houses, taverns, brandy shops and eating places, all in tents and booths. To accommodate the visitors, all the local villages took lodgers, barns were turned into taverns, and butchers and suppliers came daily from the neighbouring counties to feed the crowds.

St. Bartholomew

St. Bartholomew's Fair at Smithfield in London was primarily an entertainment fair, although you needed to be of stern stuff to relish some of the cruder, crueller entertainments. During the reign of Charles II the fair became a byword for coarse license, even though seventy special constables were appointed to keep the peace. Technically a Cloth Fair, it was for a short while, attended by the city tailors with due ceremony. But the plays and circus acts were the thing most documented by writers like Ben Jonson and Samuel Pepys. By their time, the morality plays of mediaeval times had given way to puppet plays, acrobats—and guzzling. There was an ox roasted whole, sold in steaming hot slices, roast pig in a hundred booths, and as Jonson put it:

> *There double-beer and bottled ale,*
> *In every corner had good sale.*

Another St. Bartholomew's Fayre has been revived at Newbiggen by the Sea in Northumberland at which members of the Women's Institute help out. St. Bartholomew is the patron saint of beekeepers, and at one time it was customary to harvest honey on his day. Bartlemas biscuits impressed with the saint's seal and a traditional bun were distributed to the poor and pilgrims to Canterbury.

Gingerbread stalls were always popular.

August 13

August 20

August 14

August 21

August 15

August 22

August 16

August 23

August 17

August 24
St Bartholomew

August 18

August 25

August 19

August 26

HARVEST GATHERING

Today when a great combine harvester rolls into action harvesting is swift, complete and impersonal. This was not so in the past. The length of time harvesting took depended not only on weather, but also on the strength of men's arms and wills, and the capacity of their beasts which their master dared not strain to breaking point. Hay, corn, straw, whatever the crop, men worked in a team with a traditional and unquestioning mutual urge to do their best.

Hemp seed and thread had been plucked in July, and also flax which was then set to dry. Another July crop was buckwheat, still used as breadcorn in Tudor and Stuart England. But throughout most of England the main harvesting months were August and September. It was then that the main breadcorns—barley, rye and wheat—were normally harvested, together with oats, peas and beans, although to some extent it depended on the weather and where one lived.

Since various grains were harvested, in order to deploy his men to best advantage, the farmer had to assess by eye when each would be ready. Reaping was done by hand or later by simple machine, and was then bundled or stacked by hand for carrying home to be threshed and winnowed under cover. The farmer had to judge by eye too how long the grains should stand in the stocks before being carried home on the great harvest wains. All this took experience and knowledge of the soil and land which no science could supply.

Ever since the Black Death in the fourteenth century there had been a pool of casual farm labourers. This pool was swelled in the harvest months by town dwellers whose own work virtually shut down in summer. The farmer or master would often book his band of hired helpers well ahead, perhaps even the previous year. His need of them ensured that they got reasonable treatment, for they could be independent-minded. Sometimes workers came back to the same area year after year. As they might come from miles away, they had to be housed as well as fed by the master. Whole families, with children, babes in arms and grannies would come, so there was a goodly crowd to cater for.

For the work schedule, the farmer appointed one of his own men as Harvest Lord. The Harvest Lord dictated the hours and rate of reaping for each team, and swapped the men round to prevent them getting too exhausted in heavy jobs. The women, who raked and stacked the sheaves, were in his charge too. He also saw that food and drink were on the spot when needed, and dictated the rest periods. These were generally a fifteen-minute stop half way through the morning and two similar ones in

the afternoon. There was also an hour's break at noon when workers had their dinners and could sleep.

Feeding the faggers (itinerant labourers) was a special seasonal task for the farmer's wife, and might determine whether a team would reappear next year. They needed good nourishment, and judged an employer by the quality of the 'vittles' almost as much as by the cash.

Wiltshire farmers used to give their men generous joints of bacon several times during harvest, and provided a midday meal of meat and vegetables as well as unlimited ale or beer. Bacon or bread, cheese and ale were the usual snacks at short breaks. In Herefordshire, Anne Hughes' husband John contracted with his team to feed themselves for an extra penny a day—a risky arrangement since hen run, hutch and pigsty were easy of access. However, she still had to make a meal for the faggers when they first arrived, and a modest festive one when they left, as well as the daily draughts of drink. She also provided cakes, made from enriched bread dough.

The Hughes' festive meal for the faggers consisted of meat pasties and a boiled ham, three baked fowls, baked potatoes, fruit tarts and a thick sweetened baked beestings custard with dried fruit and a cinnamon-sprinkled top. (Beestings was the extra rich first milk from the cow after giving birth.) They also got beer and

Harvest gathering was a highly organized activity.

cider. As Anne herself said, they did pretty well.

Herefordshire being cider country, these workers had great jars of cider to quench their daytime thirst. Sometimes cider or perry had the milk from a benign cow milked into it, making a cider milkshake or simple liquid syllabub. Every county or area had its preferred ale or mixed brew. Cornishmen liked to add cherries to their cider, while Kentish men made cherry beer. Herb ales had been popular until Tudor times. After that the standard harvest drink became hopped beer.

One interesting and practical harvesting custom is recorded by the nineteenth century Wiltshire poet Alfred Williams. On the Downs, it seems, farmers let their men have what they needed 'on tick' before the working season, and set the bill against their earnings. If a man spent more than he earned, a good employer let him do extra work to pay it off. Extra payments were also made in kind, much in the old feudal way. The men would get a sack of wheat or mutton at a nominal price, and bean stubble for fuel.

August 27	September 3
August 28	September 4
August 29	September 5
August 30	September 6
August 31	September 7
September 1 *St. Giles*	September 8
September 2	September 9

HARVEST END

Wherever men grew food, the end of the corn harvest was the culminating triumph of the year. The apple harvest might be later, nutting time later still, and stock would not normally be killed off for winter salting until November. But grain, and the bread and beer made from it, were men's staple source of survival and its ingathering was celebrated with joy (and perhaps relief in a poor year or in dangerous times).

No matter how they were interpreted, many harvest rituals were at their core savagely primitive, embodying man's oldest belief that the same life animated the corn as himself. It was thought that the Earth Goddess in the form of the Corn Spirit fled before the reapers' sickles and took refuge in the last standing corn. The various kinds of horse-play and mock sacrifice, which took place in the field at the cutting of the last sheaf were a remnant of the old need to placate the Earth for the destruction of the Spirit and to resurrect her to provide next year's harvest. The last sheaf was never destroyed, but was twisted into the form of a doll and carried home in triumph on the Last Load. It was then set in a place of honour at the Harvest Supper. Even today, the present writer knows an elderly countrywoman who tenderly preserves ears from one harvest to the next.

Rivalries and sacrifices were then forgotten in the real celebration of the day, the Harvest Home or Mell Supper in the garlanded farmhouse kitchen or bakehouse. The name Mell comes from the Norse word for corn. The way the harvesters worked together shows clearly why the Harvest Supper was such a real celebration, a genuinely shared festival. Nothing was stinted, neither food nor drink.

We have some of the old menus recorded in diaries. Alfred Williams mentions hams and beef being boiled for hours beforehand. There was usually a great roly-poly plum pudding or Spotted Dick, vegetables, apple pies or tarts, custards and a grand full-fat green (new) cheese still juicy enough to be eaten without being pared thin. In the Midlands and the North Country there were also a harvest cake or lardy cake, made of bread dough rich with butter or (usually) lard, and often holding dried fruit. The men drank ale, or cider in the West Country. The women might settle for cider, milk or a homemade lemonade which had a kick all its own.

After the toasts the harvest songs would be sung, each slightly different, depending on the area. The tables would be cleared and there would be dancing to fiddles and pipes or a band. Then at last everyone would wander, or reel, home.

Some years ago members of the Women's Institute recreated a Mell Supper at Rydedale. It was a huge meal. There was a large game pie, curd cheese cake, spiced loaf, apple pie eaten with cheese, boiled ham, beef, Gale Beer (made from Bog Myrtle), tea cakes and treacle tart.

Harvest Festival

Harvest Festival as we know it is a modern Christian idea, the brainchild of a Cornish vicar in 1843. The Lammastide custom of offering the first fruit was turned into a celebration and thanksgiving for all the harvest. Today, in country churches especially, Harvest Sunday sees the altar steps laden with giant vegetables, fruits, cakes and harvest loaves in the shape of sheaves. A harvest celebration was started in East Brent in Somerset in 1857. A procession led by a brass band to a combined service is followed by a lunch of cold roast boiled beef and boiled ham, plum pudding,

bread and cheese. The puddings are carried in procession by the ladies, followed by a huge loaf and a hundred-pound cheese.

Threshing Time

Threshing took place later, normally once Michaelmas was past. Flail threshing had a ritual all of its own. The floor in the centre of the great barn facing the door would be swept clean and stamped flat. The corn would be piled high on the floor so that the flails fell on a resilient mass, shaking the corn loose. The men stood in the circle, flailing in turn in an even rhythm to the leader's chant. Then the corn had to be winnowed. Everyone worked long hours, with short breaks mid-morning and mid-afternoon and a longer one at noon. Dinner consisted of bread and cheese and quantities of ale or beer, as threshing was thirsty work. If they were lucky, there was Threshing Cake—an old-fashioned dripping

Threshing came after Harvest Home.

cake. In Cumberland, Tatie Pot and Rice Pudding were traditional on threshing days.

The Straw Harvest

Then the straw, a valuable commodity in the past, had to be dealt with. Wheat or rye would be scythed short at harvest, close to the ear, and the straw was left to be cut later for fodder. For centuries labourers gave birth, and labourers were sheltered by, slept and died on straw, while everyone used it as food and litter for their beasts. Its harvesting was almost as important as that of grain itself. Straw was used for thatch, furniture and for rope. Straw rope made beehives, baskets and paliasses, beds and strong draughtproof screens, mats and chairs as well as hampers and ropes for fishermen.

September 10

September 11

September 12

September 13

September 14

September 15

September 16

September 17

September 18

September 19

September 20

September 21
St. Matthew

September 22

September 23

MICHAELMAS

Goose in the Pot

Michaelmas has always been one of the most attractive seasons of the rural year with its haunting, long-stemmed blue-mauve daisies recalling summer, and its golden stubbled fields, hopefully under mild skies before the winter storms set in. For villagers, it was a kindly time when women and children went gleaning and gathering woodland crops as free food against the winter. Michaelmas too was a great time for horse, cattle and hiring fairs up and down England. With harvest in, these fairs from Tudor times on were the one time when farmers and factors could buy and chaffer, negotiate and bargain at their ease.

There was also a proper Michaelmas Feast. A goose which had been turned onto the stubble was a delicacy prized by townsman, squire and labourer alike, not so different from the first grouse shot on the Glorious Twelfth today. Nor did they only value the goose for its flesh. Its long feathers made quill pens for clerks, and the shorter ones pastry brushes or dusters for their wives. Best of all, any country dweller except a pauper could and did bless his snuggle-deep goose feather mattress and quilt against the winter chill.

In the more remote, poorer areas, especially in rural Wales, goosemeat had always been an important festival food at any season, but never more so than at Michaelmas. Roasting was unknown in many homes, but a good-sized bird made a fine cawl or stew with onions and oatmeal eaten with mashed potatoes, if no more. Elsewhere, any wise housewife with a pot or spit to spare would usually cook an extra bird or two to make potted meat and goose pasties or pies to keep until Christmas.

Gleanings

Gleaning was an accepted social custom which might tide rural people over a bad patch, or even save them from the dreaded workhouse as recently as the early 1900's. We easily forget just how poor many rural people were in the past. As the old feudal pattern declined, and especially after the Reformation, lordly and clerical charity had dwindled with the rise of commercial agriculture. Without a regular wage the family of a sick man might have nothing at all except an occasional Church Ale handout or dole.

Many went gleaning, as the grain was a seasonal bonus. In the days of hand-reaping, a hard-working family could get enough wheat or barley in a day for Frumenty for a kind of

Fairs were a time for merrymaking as well as serious bargaining.

harvest dinner, or even for flour, if they could afford a hand quern. Francis Kilvert recorded in Herefordshire seeing 'gleaning children coming home at the edge of night with great bundles of leased wheat poised in their heads'. That was a fortnight before Michaelmas in 1871. Alfred Williams also told how his mother took her children gleaning in the harvest holidays a few years later. They had small linen bags tied round their waists for the loose ears, and each had to bring her a set number of handfuls before the day was out.

When the gleaners had finished, geese and poultry were turned onto the stubble to be fattened for the market and the Michaelmas Feast. After that, the cows would be allowed to graze off any green growth to lengthen the milking season for a while. Lastly, the straw would be cut.

Another valuable late September crop was Fern (bracken). Acorns too were gathered by children to feed the hog fattening in the sty.

Autumn Fairs

Late September and October was the year's chief time for fairs. This was the time to sell off any stock and draught animals, and to clear the shelves in the dairy and stillroom to make room for the new season's goods. Many Mop or Hiring Fairs were held now too, as farm-workers' contracts often ran from one Michaelmas to the next.

The Midlands was the great clearing house to which produce could travel from all over England. Sheep, cattle, horses, pigs, poultry and produce as well as farm gear and domestic goods all changed hands at the great Midlands fairs. At one time almost every town had a fair, but the greatest was the Bedford Michaelmas Fair. 'Here', wrote Daniel Defoe, 'is the best market for all sorts of provisions that is to be seen at any country town . . . and tho' it is so far

from London, yet the higglers or carriers buy great quantities of provisions here for London markets . . . ' and he goes on to extol its export of fine wheat.

What Defoe does not mention are the hot Warden Pears for which Bedford Fair was famous:

> *Smoking hot, piping hot.*
> *Who knows what I've got in my pot?*
> *Hot baked Wardens.*
> *All hot! All hot! All hot!*

Other special foods served at Midlands Fairs were Bower Cakes, Fruite Sweetemeetes and Gingerbread at Lichfield, Hock and Dough Flake (a port, potato and herb dumpling) at St. Luke's Fair, Wellingborough, and Banbury Cakes at any fair close to Banbury.

The best remembered fair, however, as it still survives (only as a pleasure fair) is the Nottingham Goose Fair. Not a single goose is sold alive there now, but at its height 20,000 geese are said to have walked to Nottingham at Michaelmas time.

September 24

October 1

September 25

October 2

September 26

October 3

September 27

October 4

September 28

October 5

September 29
St. Michael and All Angels

October 6

September 30

October 7

HERRINGS & OYSTERS

Herrings from Yarmouth

Autumn was a busy time for fisherfolk because their boats would soon be hauled up or might be kept at home by bad weather. At least until the seventeenth century the herring fleet especially would be working at full stretch, and workers at the ports laboured the clock round, pickling and salting fish to feed inlanders through the winter.

The herring fleets were of vital importance. Ordinary people were so dependent upon salted and dried herring and ling for fast days, that if supplies were cut off, they might even starve. Once at least, sea pirates held a government to ransom simply by blockading the land's fishing ports. Even if they had wanted to break the rules in such emergencies, it would not have helped much. In mediaeval England the farmers just did not breed enough meat animals. There had to be herring.

The port of Great Yarmouth grew rich thanks to red herrings. These were salted, then smoked, dried and re-smoked until stiff and dryish, lightweight and smoky-red. Like this they defied any bacteria or change in climate, wcrc almost unbreakable and very nearly inedible except after long soaking. Such merits made them an ideal winter food from Saxon times until refrigeration removed the need for such fare. Sailors and travellers, pilgrims and pioneers lived on them for months on end.

Fisherfolk were communities unto themselves, with their own lore and customs, suspicious of authority and of landsmen in general. They understood their own kind better, even those from foreign parts. Yet they were intensely parochial and fiercely jealous of nearby fishing fleets, because the fishing grounds open to their small boats were limited, and one fleet's catch could mean disaster for another. The story of Yarmouth Herring Fair, held between Michaelmas and Martinmas, illustrates this well.

The Herring Fair was held under a Royal Charter, and while it lasted the local fishermen's closed shop fell away. Boats from Kent and Sussex and even from across the North Sea brought in their fish freely for sale, to the town's great profit. The fair was run by six men of Yarmouth and (strangely) six men from the Cinque Ports, together with bailiffs appointed

Fishermen were vital to the mediaeval economy.

'The First Day of Oysters'. Engraving after A. Fraser.

by the Barons of the Cinque Ports. The first three weeks of the fair, which might last forty days, was a splendid time for gourmets and guzzlers. The moment the bailiffs arrived with their officers on Michaelmas Eve they were invited to a festive dinner, and this set the tone. The bailiffs kept open house, having come prepared with sixteen hogsheads of the best possible ale. At the end there was a banquet for the town notables.

The more they prospered, the more the men of Yarmouth grew to resent the intrusion of the men of the Cinque Ports. The culmination came in 1297 when they burnt each other's boats. Retribution came in a Royal Statute of Herrings, which placed the fair even more firmly under the Cinque Port's bailiffs. It was never quite the same after that, although Dutch fishermen did much to maintain Yarmouth's profits until the Dutch wars of the seventeenth century.

The trade of the sea created one pleasant folk custom. Every year on the Sunday before the fair the men of East Anglia gathered to greet a fleet of Dutch herring schuyts with their yellow sails and striped pennants, as they sailed up the Yarmouth Roads. For the whole of Dutch Sunday the baggy-breeched Dutchmen hobnobbed with the English fishermen. It was thanks to the Dutch that the men of Yarmouth learnt to make bloaters at a time when English gourmets began to demand something better than the fiercesome red herring. Yarmouth Bloaters, slightly luxurious as smoked fish go, are still justly famous.

Oysters Galore

Down the coast from Yarmouth lies Colchester, whose wealth was also based on a sea harvest. This harvest comes not from the open sea, but from oyster beds close inshore. Colchester was exporting oysters to Rome in the year 61 A.D., and her oysters have been famous throughout England as well as abroad for centuries.

The main difference between the two towns and their communities is the nature of their products. Yarmouth created a mass product for a mass market and in doing so welcomed foreigners and strangers. On the other hand, Colchester produced a gourmet product close to home. Self-sufficient and full of ancient pride, it had no need to welcome strangers to the town.

Like Yarmouth, Colchester celebrated its harvest with a culminating feast. This Colchester Oyster Feast still takes place around 20th October each year, and is described in every major British guidebook. Colchester's many civic feasts were once renowned for their splendour, but only the Oyster Feast survives.

October 8

October 15

October 9

October 16

October 10

October 17

October 11

October 18
St. Luke

October 12

October 19

October 13

October 20

October 14

October 21

HALLOWTIDE

Our Hallowe'en foods and games around the fire are relics of ancient rites belonging to the Celtic New Year or Feast of Samhain (summer end). Samhain was the start of the Celtic winter. This was a time when the barriers between the living and the dead were thought to dissolve, when the dead returned for two days, and gods and devils came among men. The dead were honoured with a feast, fires were lit on the hilltops to purify and protect the land, and many rituals, mimes and games were used to foretell the events of the coming year.

It was the time to renew farm and land tenures and service contracts, to sacrifice and then eat the farm beasts which could not be fed through the winter. The Christian Church changed only the names, not the beliefs or practices. In some parts of Europe until recently, a fire was lit and a table laid with food and drink to welcome the ancestors, and candles were put in the windows to call them home. Killing an ox or a hog, pickling, smoking and sausage-making were annual rituals in all country areas until the age of mass selling.

NUTCRACK NIGHT

Some old names for Hallowe'en refer to games with nuts and fruit. Most of these games are ancient sacrificial, purifying and divining rituals. The nuts and apples symbolized the completion of the North Country harvest, which coincided with the end of the pagan year. In Cornwall, apples were a traditional gift to children up to 1880.

A famous Eating Game is Bob-Apple. Each player, with hands tied behind him, tries to bite and hold an apple floating in a tub of water or swung on a cord in front of him. If he can secure the apple in his mouth, he eats it and will prosper throughout the coming year. A Scottish and North Country variation is to swing a treacle-smeared scone in front of the player. He is likely to get extremely sticky while trying to bite on his 'fortune'. The idea of bobbing for apples in the bucket may have derived from the old toasting bowl drink called Lamb's Wool, which originally consisted of roasted apples and pulp floating in a bowl of sweetened, spiced mulled ale.

Another apple rite involved eating an

Ducking for apples at Hallowtide.

apple at midnight while looking into a mirror and brushing one's hair. With the last bite, one's future bride or groom would appear at one's left shoulder.

As for nuts, perhaps the most popular rite was to roast two chestnuts on the bars of the fire, one for a boy and one for a girl. If they cooked without any pother, the couple would marry. If one nut exploded or fell in the fire, the marriage, if it took place, would fail. Nuts roasted in the bonfire were one of the traditional foods eaten on 1st November at celebrations of Calen Gaeaf (the first day of winter) in North Wales. White cheese and oatcakes were also eaten. In the Isle of Man 1st November was celebrated as New Year's Day up until the seventeenth century.

ALL SOULS' DAY

Until the 1860's, poor people used to go Soul Caking or Souling. The soulers would go round the village, singing an ancient Souling song and begging for charity. This was usually given in the form of real cakes as well as money. Cakes—or (earlier) spiced breads—are one of the oldest forms of gift or dole, offered in memory of the dead or in return for prayers on their behalf.

Children still went Soul Caking up until the last war, but by then Caking had come to mean just begging pennies for sweets, fireworks or oatmeal parkin. Today, the custom by adults only seems to survive at Dungworth in Yorkshire, where there is a fancy dress competition in the local pub in which everyone gets a nominal prize.

Soul Cakes and Souling Songs varied from area to area. The most usual cakes were small flattish sweet spiced buns, occasionally with caraway seeds. John Aubrey recorded in 1686 that in Shropshire the cakes were 'about the bignesse of tuppenny cakes', and were made in quantity by housewives, since every passer-by expected to be given one. In parts of Scotland, the cakes were known as Dirge Loaves, and may have been small round wheat or barley loaves, as they were around Whitby in Yorkshire, where the loaves were called Saumas Cakes. (Elsewhere in Yorkshire, Saumas Cakes were small fruit cakes.)

GUY FAWKES NIGHT

Guy Fawkes, although relatively modern, has become a folklore figure by acquiring some the Hallowtide customs such as bell ringing, the bonfire, Hallowe'en turnip lanterns and fireworks, as well as the Soulmas Parkin. In Worcestershire and Herefordshire Black Pudding used to be eaten, while in villages in Cumberland Bonfire Biscuits and Plot Toffee are still part of Guy Fawkes Night celebrations. Toffee also features in Swaledale, Yorkshire.

Guy Fawkes is a relatively modern folk figure.

October 22

October 29

October 23

October 30

October 24

October 31
Hallowe'en

October 25

November 1
All Saints' Day

October 26

November 2
All Souls' Day

October 27

November 3

October 28
SS. Simon and Jude

November 4

MARTINMAS

Taking Stock

In mediaeval England, lack of fodder was winter's overriding problem. Grass was thin and scanty, and the cultivation of root crops was not yet understood. After the straw was cut, cattle were turned onto the stubble just as pigs were driven into the woods to forage for nuts. But once winter ploughing began, stock had to be reduced to a few breeding animals. Martinmas (the Feast of St. Martin) became the time to kill off stock which could no longer be fed. Most people took the chance to overeat on the last fresh meat, and even poor folk hoped to have a meat meal.

A 1744 version of Thomas Tusser's handbook recorded that 'Martlemas beef is beef dried in the chimney, as bacon, and is so called because it was usual to kill the beef for this provision about the feast of St. Martin'. Beef and pork in particular were salted and dried or pickled in vinegar and spices, while trimmings and offals made sausages, brawns, blood puddings, faggots and similar delicacies which could be preserved in fat. There was usually plenty over for a feast or two. Scotland made more of a ceremony of feasting than other parts. There an ox, known as the Mart, was slaughtered and eaten before the rest was salted down.

Martinmas was the first day of the old pagan winter, and another reason for ritual was the submerged belief that blood must be shed, or an unlucky year would follow. Doors and the foreheads of all the household were marked with the sign of the Cross in blood, before the meat of the slaughtered animal was served at the feast.

The Martinmas Foy

In Scotland, where harvest was late, Martinmas also marked the changeover of the labour force and the ending of hiring agreements. Farm workers about to leave their employer had their own special custom. After the horses were fed and the stable closed on Martinmas Eve, they gave a supper of bread and cheese, with whisky to drink, to those staying behind. Music, singing and dancing followed, probably keeping the farmer and his family awake. About a week later, the stay-behinds in their turn gave a similar feast for any newcomers.

Courts and Rights

Many Martinmas ceremonies are connected with the organization of community matters and the payment of dues to establish and assert grazing or similar rights. In ancient times a community worked together by custom in two main ways. First, as a group, people held and maintained the right to graze cattle or sheep or to let pigs forage in certain areas of common land, no matter who owned them. Pigs provided peasants with their main winter meat. Second, people farmed the land communally, working side by side in strips, instead of

owning individual fields.

After the Norman Conquest land was divided into administrative units called manors. The lord of the manor had the right to hold a Court Leet. Here, he or his steward dealt with disputes and his bailiffs punished minor offences. A wise and humane lord realized the worth of a loyal work force and ruled largely by co-operation. He respected for instance the villagers' ancient rights of grazing their beasts on what was now his land. A few Court Leets and similar community meetings survive today, with fascinating or comic ancient features.

Laxton in Nottinghamshire is the only place in England where strip farming is still practised. There are three fields making 383 acres of arable land and 47 acres of sykes (grass verges of streams). On Jury Day, sometime during November, twelve elected men set out from a pub to inspect the fields and sykes, and note anyone who has nabbed extra land. They then go back to the pub for lunch, to draw up a report with a list of fines to be paid. The actual Court meets a week or two later. Of the money collected from fines, half goes to the Minister of Agriculture, who is now Lord of the Manor, and the other half, needless to say, is earmarked to pay for next year's Jury Feast.

The Duke of Buccleugh is Lord of the Knightlow Hundred in Warwickshire, probably an older land division than the fields of Laxton. It does not rate a Court Leet, but every year before sunrise on 11th November, representatives of the parishes gather at a large stone in a field near Dunchurch, the remains of Knightlow Cross. The Duke's agent reads a Charter of Assembly, and requires everyone to drop his tithe into a hollow in the stone, saying 'Wroth Silver'. This payment originally gave parishioners the right to drive their cattle over Dunsmore Hill, and is still strictly enforced. Afterwards the company have a slap-up breakfast at the local inn paid for by the Duke, and they drink his health in rum and milk.

The officers of the Wareham Court Leet in Dorset once inspected seriously the local hostelries. The inspection has now become a comic pub-crawl enjoyed immensely by the townspeople. The officers go on their tour accompanied by ale-tasters, bread-weighers, chimney sweeps and a constable in true mediaeval style. Everyone visited gets fined. The landlord gives short measure and laces his beer. The bread is heavy—hardly surprising, since it may hide a bottle of liquor. The chimneys are dirty. It is all good fun, with vivid repartee from both sides. The Court meets the following week to hear a serious report on the condition of Wareham Common and to let out the grazing rights for the year. Before electing the new officers, there is a grand traditional midday dinner.

Martinmas was the first day of the old pagan winter.

November 5
Guy Fawkes

November 12

November 6

November 13

November 7

November 14

November 8

November 15

November 9

November 16

November 10

November 17
St. Hugh

November 11
St. Martin

November 18

ST CLEMENT'S DAY

St. Clement could be expected to be popular with the men, for he was one of the seamen's saints as well as the patron saint of blacksmiths. Smiths celebrated his day with much noise and guzzling. They were given to exploding gunpowder on their anvils and similar practices. In many places including Twyford in Hampshire they held a Clem Feast in the evening. Dockyard smiths especially liked celebrating. A figure called Old Clem was carried through the streets, and stopped in the pubs to hand round a collecting box for contributions for the supper which would end the evening.

Bakers too celebrated St. Clements Day, and in Cambridge they used to have a communal meal. In Tenby boat-owners gave their crews a roast goose and rice pudding supper. Inland, the day was more of an apple and pear feast. Throughout Staffordshire it was called Bite-Apple Day, and the same games were played as at Hallowtide. At Walsall, apples and nuts or hot pennies were thrown from the Guildhall to be scrambled for. At Ripon, the Cathedral choristers offered the congregation apples stuck with sprigs of box in return for a small dole.

But it was to children that St. Clement really seemed to belong. Clementing was a clearly recognized and accepted form of children's begging up to the end of the last century. Their verses similar to Shrovetide songs, were more like a demand than pleading. For example:

Clemany! Clemany! Clemany mine!
A good red apple and a pint of wine,
Some of your mutton and some of your
*   veal;*
If it is good, pray give me a deal;
If it is not, pray give me some saut,
Butler, butler, fill your bowl,
If though fillest it of the best,
The Lord'll send your soul to rest;
If though fillest it of the small,
Down goes butler, bowl and all;
Pray good mistress send to me,
One for Peter, one for Paul,
One for Him who made us all;
Apple, pear, plum or cherry;
Any good thing to make us merry;
A bouncing buck and a velvet chair.
Clement comes but once a year;
Off with the pot and on with the pan,
A good red apple and I'll be gone.

ST CATHERINE'S DAY

Lacemakers in particular venerated St. Catherine The main lacemaking counties were Bedford, Buckingham, Cambridge, Hertford, Huntingdon and Northampton. However, Bedfordshire was the centre of this important cottage industry, largely because St. Catherine became confused with Queen Catherine of Aragon who lived at Ampthill Park just before her divorce from Henry VIII. The queenly association persisted, even up to 1956 when pattern of lace called Catherine of Aragon's lace was still being made

Children always joined in the fun and games on St Caterine's Day and St. Andrew's Day.

in the Leighton Buzzard area.

In Buckinghamshire the St. Cat's Day holiday began with the local bellman bellowing out on his rounds:

Rise, maids, rise!
Bake your cattern pies.
Bake enough and bake no waste,
And let the bellman have a taste.

During the day the women went visiting, singing their working songs, and were entertained with wiggs, made from one of the usual recipes but flavoured with caraway. They also got warm ale or beer laced with rum and thickened with egg yolks—all luxuries for such poor people.

The girls would play games on St. Cat's Day, but older workers, as a rule, held a more sober ceremony called Wetting the Candle Block. This derived from the fact that from this date onward, working by candlelight (or rather rushlight in most cases) was allowed until February when the days lengthened.

The simplest form of the Wetting ceremony consisted of setting up a candle-steel and a single lighted tallow candle on a table or wooden block surrounded by glasses filled with water, which condensed the candlelight. By this means one candle could be made to light the work of four or six workers instead of just one. Once the candle-block was set up, the group had tea and ate Cattern Cake. This was an enriched bread dough, raised with brewer's yeast, and containing lard, egg, sugar, caraway seeds, and sometimes mashed potato. A piece of the dough might sometimes be set aside to make a Tanders Cake five days later. The Cattern Tea was sometimes followed by a game called Leap Candle, and later by an apple-pie supper.

ST ANDREW'S DAY

Andermas, as St. Andrew's Day was often called, was a great Scottish feast day and holiday. Boys would go hunting rabbits and squirrels in the morning for the Andermas Feast, and then turn to good cheer. They still do. Haggis is still the main dish, messy to make, but savoury and satisfying to eat, with malt whisky always the chief drink.

In some parts of England St. Andrew rivalled St. Catherine as the saint of lacemakers. Tanders or Tandry Day was a time of

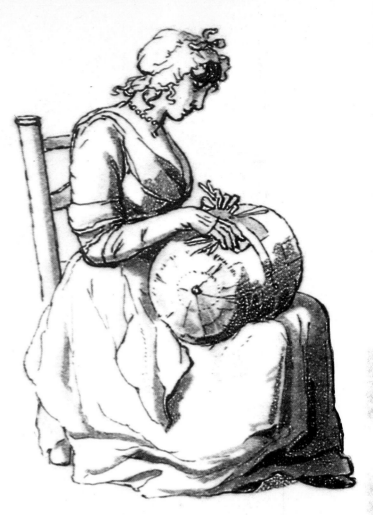

general merriment and good eating. Men and women exchanged clothes and went visiting, usually to drink hot elderberry wine and to eat Tanders Cake. This was sometimes a piece of Cattern Cake. At Olney in Buckinghamshire, they drank Metheglyn (spiced mead) with toast floating in it, taken with Thrumety (frumenty) and sweets called No-Candy.

Tanders Day was a time for overturning the rules too. For instance the Lace School children at Stratton, Northamptonshire used to lock out their mistress with a traditional song. In other places the lacemakers' form of Bob Apple was played.

A modern revival of the Cattern Tea or an apple-pie supper and games combining the Cattern and Tanders customs might be a pleasant way to lighten the dark November evenings or to raise funds for Christmas charities now that Advent has started.

November 19

November 26

November 20

November 27

November 21

November 28

November 22
St. Cecilia

November 29

November 23
St. Clement

November 30
St. Andrew

November 24

December 1

November 25
St. Catherine

December 2

CHRISTMAS PREPARATIONS

Stirring Up Christmas

All over England on Stir Up Sunday—the Sunday before Advent—some families still gather round the big bowl in which the Christmas Pudding lies glistening. Each member, even the smallest, gives the mixture at least a token stir, and makes a silent wish for blessing. The idea behind the custom is that the whole household should join in preparing for the year's most joyous festival.

This custom is quite a modern one, because the special association of Plum Pudding with Christmas only dates back to about 1836. But the pudding itself, like other boiled puddings, had been popular since 1617 when the pudding cloth was invented. Before that, so-called puddings were stuffings or else starchy, spiced mixtures boiled in a bladder like a haggis.

The real forerunner of Christmas Pudding was a meat pottage or soup, thickened with breadcrumbs and egg, flavoured with spices and dried fruit, and coloured bright red. It was called unromantically Stewed Broth, and it began its climb to fame in late Tudor times when prunes were first added to boiled mixtures. These dried plums were so popular that they gave their name to all other dried fruits. Thus curranty breads and cakes became plum cakes, and Stewed Broth became Plum Pottage.

Soon, with the opening up of the New World and Eastern trading posts, dried fruits and sugar became cheap enough to make Plum Pottage a festival dish, even for the poor. Now a more solid, richer mixture or porridge, it changed its name again to Plum or Christmas Porridge. As such, well thickened, it became one of the first candidates for boiling in a bag or cloth.

The first cloth-boiled plum puddings seem to have contained no alcohol. However, George I on his first Christmas Day in England was served a rich Plum Pudding which had lost its meat, but kept its suet and had gained a large wineglass of brandy. In 1806 Mrs. Maria Rundell put a recipe for Common Plum Pudding with wine in it among her meat puddings. Ten years later, Dr. William Kitchiner created a Plum Pudding with brandy as—of all things—a Lenten dish. Far from being exclusively a Christmas treat, a handsome Plum Pudding had come to crown every parish feast or Harvest Home, tithe dinner or wedding breakfast.

Both rich and poor enjoyed Plum Pudding at Christmas. The pudding could be boiled in a pot over the family fire, so was cheap on fuel. It was a big treat to supplement the poor man's usually meagre beef or goose. It was in this role that Charles Dickens saw it. Good journalist that he was, he wrote it up as the central symbol of Christmas cheer and plenty, and found a receptive audience. The new urban middle class was seeking to recreate what they believed had been mediaeval Christmas revelry. Moreover, the concept and the dish were just to the taste of the young Queen Victoria's husband, Prince Albert. So Christmas Pudding became what we know it today.

Preparing for Christmas. Painting by F. Hardy.

that to give to women in this way signified that goodwill demanded by the Stir Up Sunday collect. Perhaps too, they had a sense that no woman should be turned away without help at this season, as the Mother of God had been.

There is a delightful description of Thomassing in Surrey during the nineteenth century. 'Mr. Daniel Simmonds of Rodsall distributed to each (woman) a Gain of rye, which was ground for them gratuitously by Mrs. Valler of Cutt Mill. Some of them made pancakes of the meal, and otherwise employed it in their Xmas festivities. John Winter remembers the old women of Puttenham (many of them in red cloaks with hoods over their bonnets) trotting about on St. Thomas' Day, bent on collecting their Goodings'.

Wassailing

Wassailing the apple orchards was just one of the very old customs practised at the Christmas season. It took place in the fruit-growing counties of the West Country and the South-East, often on Christmas Eve. The farmer and his men would carry a pail or Wassail Bowl of hot mulled cider to the trees, and splash it around the roots of the most fruitful one. A cake or bread dipped in cider was hung on a branch, and the tree was then toasted with a song, both as a warning and an encouragement to bear well next year. Horns were blown, trays were banged, and a general hullabaloo ended the ritual to drive away the evil spirits.

Wassailing was originally the pledge of peace and protection implied in drinking a toast or health. It was usual to carry a filled Wassail Bowl to one's neighbours before Christmas to wish them well. In time, youngsters took to going round with a beribboned but empty bowl, to sing goodwill songs in return for gifts of food or cash. This in turn paved the way for modern carol-singing.

Another form of seeking alms took place on St. Thomas' Day. The custom was called Thomassing or Mumping, and was practised only by women. Even the well-off, who would not have dreamed of begging at other times, sought and received mainly ingredients for Christmas baking. Householders seemed to feel

December 3

December 10

December 4

December 11

December 5

December 12

December 6
St. Nicholas

December 13

December 7

December 14

December 8

December 15

December 9

December 16

CHRISTMASTIDE

Midwinter Celebrations

In early England, Christmastide was a twelve-day holiday. Preparations had been made weeks before, laying in supplies and making preservable foods. Christmas Day itself was dominated by the great processional services of the Church which began at midnight. But in rural areas where hints of the practices of a more ancient pagan midwinter festival survived, cleansing and fortune-telling rites took place on Christmas Eve. There might also be a sturdy supper before the midnight churchgoing.

One of the main features of the Christmas Eve supper was Frumenty. Frumenty is perhaps man's most ancient dish, quite likely dating back to before the Iron Age. It consists of cree'd hulled wheat, stewed very gently for twelve hours or more, then boiled if necessary until it jellies. Mixed with milk, sweetened and spiced, it can either be eaten hot as a porridge, or cold with cream as a dessert.

The rich ate Frumenty all the year round with venison, a festive meat, or with porpoise, the equivalent of venison for fast days. The poor ate it by itself, sweetened, and with a few currants and spices. In many parts of England, as in Leicestershire it was eaten throughout the winter hunting season, or as in Dorset, at mid-Lent or Easter.

In the North and East, especially in Yorkshire, Lincolnshire and Suffolk, Frumenty is a traditional Christmas dish with a history spanning at least two thousand years. Around Whitby it was eaten with gingerbread and several Women's Institute members report that it is still a Christmas Eve treat in Yorkshire. In Suffolk, it was eaten within living memory throughout the twelve days, and a little was put outside the back door nightly for the *Pharisees* (fairies).

Miss A.R. Burkett has described the traditional candlelit Christmas Eve meal in the Yorkshire Dales. Following the Frumenty there were Yule Cakes (a type of Hot Cross Bun recipe) eaten cold with butter and cheese. In other places the Yule Log was lit in the hearth, the Yule candle stood on the table, and the family would drink Lamb's Wool, the ancient

Many Christmas feasts and revels were held in mediaeval manor halls.

drink of mulled ale which had roasted apple pulp added.

At Mousehole in Cornwall, fishermen used to hold a special Christmas Eve feast, where they ate seven different sorts of fish. A popular hot Christmastide drink in Cornwall was Shenagrum, made of beer, rum, sugar and spice. In Surrey, hot Elder Wine gave rise to much merriment.

Christmas Feasts

In mediaeval times a feast was held in manor halls. All the household officials and workers would attend, and the whole event would be formally regulated. The centrepiece might be a peacock in his feathers with gilded beak, or a boar's head. There might be other *grete fowles* such as bustard or swan.

By Tudor times, boars and bustards had almost disappeared. Providentially, it seems, the break with Rome led to a big increase in cattle rearing, and so roast beef soon became every Englishman's festive dish throughout the

year. Turkeys were first seen in England about 1542, and by the 1590's had become a popular feast food on every comfortable man's table. By the end of the eighteenth century, Norwich was sending a thousand turkeys a day up to London, and still more at Christmas time. Nevertheless, turkey did not replace goose or a bit of beef on the poor man's Christmas board until around the year 1900.

Mince pies were standard Christmas fare from Elizabethan days. Dish tarts—what we call plate pies—had then recently come in, made of a new, rich buttery pastry, soon to be called puff paste. These flat double crust tarts were called shred or minced pies, after their spiced shredded meat filling mixed with suet, dried fruit, orange and lemon peel and sugar.

Samuel Pepys mentions mince pies five times, and even records bustling out to buy them for his wife when she was ill. In the early 1700's it was discovered that the ingredients for mince pies could be mixed some months before Christmas, if well laced with brandy or sack, and if the meat were only added at the last moment. Soon thereafter it became convenient to forget the meat altogether.

In the eighteenth century James Woodeforde provided the fellows of his Oxford college with cod, beef and a great plum cake, as well as mince pies. An affluent farmer at the time might provide for his household both roast and boiled beef, ham, hare and rabbit pies, goose, chickens, mince pies, apple pies, cakes and several fruit wines. In Cumberland such a man might give two dinners, one for married folk, and one for the 'singles'. In the North, the cakes would include Yule Cakes, breads or Doos, which were yeast-raised and rich with fruit and spice. These were eaten hot with mulled wine and Wensleydale cheese, or in Derbyshire with the special Christmas sage cheese. In Scotland, they were replaced by special Christmas bannocks. As for our modern Christmas feast, this derives largely from the showmanship of the royal chefs in the 1840's, augmented by later commercial enterprises.

December 17

December 18

December 19

December 20

December 21
St. Thomas

December 22

December 23

December 24

December 25
Christmas Day

December 26
St. Stephen

December 27

December 28

December 29

December 30

December 31

NEW YEAR'S EVE

Celebrating the turn of the year is a very ancient idea. Until 1752, the official New Year began on 25th March with the approach of Spring. But it was always ignored, because people were busy with sowing and lambing then. The start of the New Year was therefore made to coincide with the old Roman feast of the Kalendae Januarii and the last fling of the old Norse Yuletide. Both were age-old excuses for a good carousal, and took place conveniently during the farmworkers' midwinter break.

When the Protestant reformers stopped people from enjoying the non-religious traditions of Christmas, the idea of making New Year's Eve an eating and drinking spree got extra point, especially in Scotland. It was no hardship to delay celebrations for just six days. From the earliest times, people believed that New Year's Eve was a time for keeping the evil spirits at bay. So the idea of welcoming the New Year with a feast intended to bribe the spirit world to bring good fortune was not forgotten. Nor was the associated idea of burning out or destroying the past in order to make a fresh start. In fact the Scots word for New Year, Hogmanay, probably has this concept behind it.

The spirits were often bribed at second-hand by presenting food gifts or other charity to visitors or beggars at one's door. One innocent, but now forgotten, Scots custom of this kind, was for children to go from house to house in a crocodile, covered with a sheet like a panto-mime dragon, and demand a Hogmanay, usually cheese and oatcakes.

Another Scots custom, recorded by Dr. Johnson on his visit to the Western Isles, was more directly linked with ancient animal worship of sacrifice. It also had features reminiscent of the Welsh New Year parade of the Mari Lwyd. Highland Scots would dress one of their number in a cow-hide, and chase him round the village, thwacking him. They would stop at various doors, and be let in for a drink. Once inside, the leader would give the house-holder a stick with a strip of animal-skin wrapped round it, which he would place in the fire. The smouldering brand would then be passed to each member of the family to sniff as a cleansing rite against evil forces.

Similarly, some Highland families would send a trusted member to a local ford or well after sunset of New Year's Eve to fetch a scoop of water and some juniper boughs. This was done in complete silence. Next morning, the water was sipped by everyone, or sprinkled on the homestead's fittings as a cleansing agent. The boughs would then be set smouldering to smoke out any evil spirits.

In the less remote villages and towns of Scotland, folk would gather near the church or market cross. Carrying jugs or buckets of the traditional Hogmanay drink Het Pint, they would perform the cleansing by burning tar barrels or lighting bonfires while making merry. Het Pint was a hot ale posset and whisky.

All over Scotland, but especially in rural

areas, the other main Hogmanay drink was made from sowans. Oatmeal sids (the vitamin-filled inner husks of the grain) were steeped in water for about a week until sour, then sieved to get rid of their bran. The starchy sediment—the sowans—was normally made into a porridge and eaten with cream and honey, or might be dried to make light pancakes. At Hogmanay the slightly fermented gruel was simply diluted and drunk.

As for Hogmanay food, oatcakes were eaten with cheeses from which Dunlop and Islay have now developed. Ankerstocks, which were round ryemeal spiced loaves, were used as New Year gingerbread. Treacle bannocks were also eaten. In more modern times, Shortbread decorated with flaked almonds and pink icing became popular. The Black Bun also might be cut during the evening; otherwise it was left for the First Footing after midnight.

Bells and Tar Barrels

England had its own New Year's Eve rituals. Church bells pealed in every village, muffled at first to mark the death of the Old Year before a clarion peal welcomed in the New Year. Bellringers usually got good liquor for their labour, possibly the English version of Het Pint. This was sweetened beer and milk, spiced and laced with spirits. In East Anglia, spiced elderberry wine was drunk while eating the triangular blessing cakes called Kitchels.

At Allendale, a remote village in Northumberland, they still hold an exciting Tar Barrel Parade. There are thirty or so participants known as Guisers, wearing elaborate costumes and preceded by a brass band. They parade through the village, each carrying a barrel full of burning tar shavings on his head, to a public bonfire. The men have to wear small bags of sand on their heads to keep off the intense heat, but very rarely has a Guiser not succeeded in reaching the bonfire. At midnight, the Church bells ring out, the band plays 'Auld Lang Syne', while friends and strangers join hands and sing. Then it is off to the First Footing, ending for some, with breakfast at an outlying farm.

INDEX

ACKNOWLEDGEMENTS

Maggie Black and Imogen Bright would like to thank everyone who has given us help with this book.

All the members and friends of the WI who have written to us, in particular Audrey Bemrose of Bridlington, East Yorkshire; Miss A.R. Burkett now of Allesley, West Midlands; E.O. Armstrong of Ripon; Margaret L. Gray of Habberley, Worcestershire; Joan Frater of Sleights, Yorkshire; Anthea M. Kenyon of Hallaton, Leicestershire; Dorothy Makin of Keighley, Yorkshire; Margaret Puntow of Woodhorn with Newbiggin, Northumbria; D.M. Swales of Appleton le Moors, Yorkshire; Dorothy Towler of Pooley Bridge, Cumbria and the members from Northumbria who wrote about carlins.

We are extremely grateful to all the county archivists and librarians who have provided us with information and helped to check our facts.

We should also like to thank Dorothy Handcock of Allendale, Northumbria; Guinness Superlatives Ltd; Richard Sharp of Jesus College, Oxford; Mrs. Carew Hunt of Westbury, Wiltshire; Penguin Books Ltd, publishers of 'The Diary of a Farmer's Wife'; The Headmaster's Secretary, Westminster School, London; The Rev. K.E. Wood, Grasmere, Cumbria; Gwen Watkins for permission to print part of 'The Ballad of the Mari Lwyd' and the scholars of folklore whose writings we have consulted. The Welsh material owes much to the good will and scholarship of Mrs. Bobby Freeman.

Photographic acknowledgements: Courtauld Institute of Art; Christies; Ben Freeman; National Gallery of Scotland; Northamptonshire Libraries; Oxfordshire County Libraries; Sotheby's; Eileen Tweedy; University of Reading, Institute of Agricultural History and Museum of Rural Life; Victoria and Albert Museum and the present owner of 'The Tichborne Dole'.